Children's Live-Action Musical Films

McFarland Classics

Children's Live-Action Musical Films

A Critical Survey and Filmography

by
Thomas J. Harris

McFarland & Company, Inc., Publishers
Jefferson, North Carolina, and London

The present work is a reprint of the library bound edition of Children's Live-Action Musical Films: A Critical Survey and Filmography, first published in 1989. McFarland Classics is an imprint of McFarland & Company, Inc., Publishers, Jefferson, North Carolina, who also published the original edition.

Library of Congress Cataloguing-in-Publication Data

Harris, Thomas J., 1966–
    Children's live-action musical films : a critical survey and
filmography / by Thomas J. Harris.
        p.   cm.
    Includes bibliographical references and index.
    ISBN 0-7864-1180-5 (softcover : 50# alkaline paper) ∞
    1. Musical films—United States—History and criticism.
    2. Children's films—History and criticism.   I. Title.
    PN1995.9.M86H38   2001   791.43'657—dc20   89-42719

British Library cataloguing data are available

On the cover: Peter Ostrum as Charlie Bucket in Willy Wonka and
the Chocolate Factory (1971)

Manufactured in the United States of America

McFarland & Company, Inc., Publishers
   Box 611, Jefferson, North Carolina 28640
   www.mcfarlandpub.com

for the myriad talented persons
who created the many cherished moments
found in these films:
you are the music-makers,
you are the dreamers of the dreams

Acknowledgments

Needless to say, this book has been a labor of love for me, since by writing about some of the films I've always loved I had the opportunity to meet some of the people who made them. I thank them for sharing their opinions of their work with me: Leslie Bricusse, Ken Hughes, Richard Fleischer, Mel Stuart, David Seltzer, Joey Walsh, Peter Lind Hayes, Dr. Seuss, Dee Dee Wood, Howard Jeffrey, Peter Ostrum, Bryan Forbes, Si Rose, Walter Scharf.

For stills, Mary Corliss & Co. at the Museum of Modern Art, Collectors Book Store in Hollywood, Jerry Ohlinger's in Manhattan, Ken Hughes and Doug McClelland. I also thank Heidi Friedman and Robin Carroll-Mann at Summit (N.J.) Public Library for their patience and help with research.

And to Maureen, Don, Joe and my family, thanks for being you.

Table of Contents

Introduction

The immediate inclination of most persons confronting the subject of this study might be to ask why I have chosen such an obviously esoteric topic for discussion — why not children's films in general? First of all, the latter is simply too broad a genre for any in-depth, film-by-film survey; indeed, one could stretch all the way back to the silent era and find, perhaps, one or two entries *per year* for examination. The inevitable unwieldiness of such a volume (which would, no doubt, reach encyclopedic length) would necessarily preclude the sort of lengthy consideration (20 pages plus) which are given to the films in this volume — and many of those early features (countless silent versions of *Alice in Wonderland, Little Women* and the like) would hardly merit a discussion of even half that length.

A recent (1983) collection of essays edited by one Douglas Street, assistant professor of English and Theater at Texas A & M University, titled *Children's Novels and the Movies,* ultimately discloses the futility of its original goal in its "selected filmography" at the end, wherein it lists approximately 100 film versions of children's books — only 30 of which it attempts to discuss in any detail. The essays range from very good to poor — not only because of their length (five pages maximum in most cases) but because the authors, not knowing the actual facts behind the production of such features as *Chitty Chitty Bang Bang* and *Willy Wonka and the Chocolate Factory* (two of the films included in this study also), for example, have made glaring inaccuracies in attributions and have, as a result, produced insubstantial writings. It has been my intention throughout this volume to clear up such misunderstandings by including statements (obtained firsthand in most cases) from the people who made the films.

A second reason for my choosing this particular topic for discussion is the fact that it marks a merging of two very popular genres. But, perhaps most importantly, I am embarking on this particular road precisely because it had been so poorly traversed in the past. In short, I sympathize with the fates of many of the films discussed here, mainly because they have taken such a bad rap over the years, having been dismissed as inferior entertainments without even having been given a fair shake. The existing articles on 90 percent of them do not extend beyond the initial, superficial theatrical reviews. (This is not to say that I have not been severe in my judgments, however, for I certainly have.) Since they continue to reach ever-increasing numbers of children (and adults, for that matter) with perennial TV screenings over the holiday seasons, a serious consideration of their merits and faults is long overdue. Every film critic, it seems, has his own theory as to what a good children's film should be, but very, very few have ever taken the time to express their thoughts on the subject in detail.

The reader will note that no animated features have been included, and nothing even remotely connected with science fiction has been touched upon—there exist already countless reference books on both genres. The 17 features included in this volume reflect the major efforts in this field since the advent of sound. All the expected entries are here—*The Wizard of Oz, Hans Christian Andersen, Mary Poppins, Willy Wonka and the Chocolate Factory*—along with less well-known items such as *The 5000 Fingers of Dr. T.* All of the films are discussed in relation to one another also—thus I will explain why *Chitty Chitty Bang Bang, Bedknobs and Broomsticks, Slipper and the Rose* and *Pete's Dragon* are largely failed attempts to recapture the magic of *Mary Poppins.*

Because many of the films were based on original screenplays and were not adaptations of books, and also since I want to accord each one the same level of treatment, each is discussed solely on the basis of its merits as a *film* and not as a literary adaptation (though in some cases I have noted changes made from page to screen in order to give a better understanding of the working methods and personalities of the individual filmmakers). Most if not all of the directors and writers of these features — men like Victor Fleming, Charles Vidor, George Pal, Robert Stevenson, Richard Fleischer, Leslie Bricusse, Ken Hughes and Bryan Forbes — are largely neglected talents whose impact on the various films are illustrated in depth for the first time.

It is my hope that after studying these critiques, the reader will be prompted to go back and take another look at aspects of these features to which he may not have given even a second glance the first time around. In that event, I shall consider that I have not embarked upon this undertaking in vain.

The Wizard of Oz

A Metro-Goldwyn-Mayer Presentation, *released by* Loews, Inc., 1939. A Victor Fleming Production. *Producer* Mervyn LeRoy. *Director* Victor Fleming. *Screenplay* Noel Langley, Florence Ryerson and Edgar Allan Woolf. *Adaptation by* Noel Langley, *from the book by* L. Frank Baum. *Musical Adaptation* Herbert Stothart. *Associate Musical Conductor* George Stoll. *Orchestral and Vocal Arrangements* George Bassman, Murray Cutter, Paul Marquardt, Ken Darby. *Editor* Blanche Sewell. *Choreography* Bobby Connolly. *Director of Photography (in Technicolor)* Harold Rosson, A.S.C. *Associate* Allen Davey, A.S.C. *Technicolor Color Director* Natalie Kalmus. *Associate* Henri Jaffa. *Recording Director* Douglas Shearer. *Art Director* Cedric Gibbons. *Associate* William A. Horning. *Set Decorations* Edwin B. Willis. *Special Effects* Arnold Gillespie. *Costumes* Adrian. *Character Makeups* Jack Dawn. *Running Time* 101 minutes.

Cast Judy Garland (Dorothy), Frank Morgan (Professor Marvel/Wizard), Ray Bolger (Hunk/Scarecrow), Bert Lahr (Zeke/Cowardly Lion), Jack Haley (Hickory/Tin Man), Billie Burke (Glinda), Margaret Hamilton (Miss Gulch/Wicked Witch), Charley Grapewin (Uncle Henry), Pat Walshe (Nikko, the head Winged Monkey), Clara Blandick (Auntie Em), Toto (Toto), the Munchkins.

Songs "Over the Rainbow," "Ding-Dong! The Witch Is Dead," "Off to See the Wizard," "If I Only Had a Brain/a Heart/the Nerve," "You're Out of the Woods," "If I Were King of the Forest," music by Harold Arlen, lyrics by E.Y. Harburg.

> "*The Wizard of Oz* remains agelessly wonderful. Some sort of magical enchantment must have fallen over MGM when they produced this film, which is made up of so many parts that are all exactly right."—*Roger Ebert*

It may come as a shock to the reader that, although *The Wizard of Oz*—celebrating its 50th birthday in 1989, certainly an

1

occasion which will prompt much fanfare—is easily the most famous and revered entry in the genre of children's musicals (and, indeed, the most well-loved motion picture in the history of the business—it has been seen by more people than any other film, with the exception of *Gone with the Wind*), there exists only a handful of articles on the film itself (as opposed to essays comparing it to the Baum novel). Apart from the original 1939 reviews, the best offerings are contemporary ones: Ray Bolger's "*The Wizard of Oz* and the Golden Era of the American Musical Film" in the February 1978 issue of *American Cinematographer,* "*The Wizard of Oz*" by Irene Kahn Atkins in *Maghill's Survey of Cinema,* Vol. 4, published in 1980, and, most recently, Robert Winning's one-page critique in *The International Dictionary of Films and Filmmakers,* published in 1984.

Without a doubt, this discrepancy derives at least in part from the fact that, because *Oz* was a product of the studio era, it was the end result of the contributions of countless combinations of individuals, many of whom did not receive final screen credit for their work. Discussing *Oz* in depth would therefore prove frustrating to many modern critics accustomed to dissecting a film (more often than not inaccurately) according to the "auteur theory" and other established tenets of film criticism. The reader may not be surprised to learn that in a letter to this author, Pauline Kael, who has been a major figure in the field for over 25 years, stated (much to her astonishment) that in all that time she had never once written about *Oz* (although she planned to say a few words in her review of 1985's *Return to Oz*)! *The Wizard of Oz,* to put it simply, was made in an era when movies were viewed as purely escapist entertainment and nothing more—which is not to say, however, that it does not have serious claims to fame as a work of cinema art—one of the main goals of this chapter is to confirm that very fact.

Fortunately for millions of devoted *Oz* fans, two recent books (both published in 1976, coincidentally, and both still in print) have been put out on the making of the film. Both of these have aided immeasurably in satisfying the moviegoer's curiosity as to the intricacies of the production. They are Doug McClelland's *Down the Yellow Brick Road: The Making of "The*

Miss Gulch (Margaret Hamilton) prepares to take Toto away. Clara Blandick and Charley Grapewin look on.

Wizard of Oz" (Pyramid Books) and Aljean Harmetz's *The Making of "The Wizard of Oz"* (Knopf). The second is infinitely preferable to the first, richly detailed and exhaustively researched, covering every possible area (it devotes separate chapters to the scripts, the directors, accidents on the set, etc.) with amazing accuracy and clarity. McClelland's rather thin (159 pages as opposed to Harmetz's 329) edition seems at first glance to be more of a treasure-trove of stills than anything else, but it offers many acute observations and little-known production details, as well as quotations from actors and technical personnel.

Between both of these landmark volumes, virtually anything the *Oz* aficionado might want to learn about the behind-the-scenes production of the film can be gleaned. For that reason, the format of this chapter on *Oz* will differ slightly from that of subsequent chapters in that neither the plot summary will be given

(anyone who is not intimately acquainted with the plot of the movie must surely be living on Mars) nor much background information — nor will there be discussion of how the film version of *Oz* compares to its literary source; that has been done countless times before. In the case of *Oz*, it is only the aesthetics of the film itself which interest me; both the McClelland and Harmetz books, for all their superb detail about the production, provide little more than superficial speculations about the artistic aspects of the finished product. In the interests of space, a knowledge of both the McClelland and Harmetz books is presupposed when discussing certain aspects of *Oz* (such as the nature of sequences like "The Jitterbug" which were eliminated from the release print).

Because *Oz* is used here as a standard of comparison for all the subsequent features, my task from this point on will be to construct a theory of what an ideal children's musical-fantasy film should be, discuss by what means (writing, direction, performances, etc.) *Oz* proves itself to be the perfect embodiment of that ideal, and lastly (and most extensively — this aspect will cover the rest of the book) illustrate how the sixteen subsequent features fail in varying degrees) to live up to the standard set by *Oz*.

Without a doubt, what distinguishes *The Wizard of Oz* most of all is its recognizing the fundamental importance of incorporating the most basic formulae of the two genres (children's story and musical film) of which it is an exponent — and its achieving, as a result, a blend of fun and fancy which appeals to adults and young people simultaneously.

Foremost among the conventions of a children's film is the necessity of establishing a child's point-of-view. In order to get a child interested in a story, he or she must be encouraged to identify and sympathize with someone in the tale who is a peer in both age and emotional temperament. This is accomplished in the opening sepia sequence through a combination of pointed dialogue and subtle direction. Our first glimpse of Dorothy (Judy

Opposite: *Glinda (Billie Burke) introduces Dorothy to the inhabitants of Munchkinland.*

Garland) running down a dirt road toward home sets up her whole character: she is a young girl (probably about eleven or twelve years of age) who, typically, feels that her existence is being threatened (in this case, she fears for the life of her dog, Toto—"Did she [Miss Gulch] hurt you? She tried to, didn't she?") and seeks assistance from her elders ("Come on—we'll go tell Auntie Em and Uncle Henry").

Director King Vidor (who was responsible for the opening and closing sections of the film) employs long takes with little cutting here in order to emphasize Dorothy's shared kinship with her aunt and uncle (Clara Blandick, Charley Grapewin) and the three farmhands, Hunk (Ray Bolger), Hickory (Jack Haley) and Zeke (Bert Lahr). We notice that while Dorothy is explaining her problem to Hunk, for example, both of them are framed in a two-shot. However, when Hunk suggests a solution ("You'd think you didn't have any brains at all. When you go home don't go *by* Miss Gulch's place") he is isolated in the frame (the same principle applies for Zeke and his "Aw, have a little courage, that's all"). Because the farmhands are depicted in this fashion, their advice seems distant, incomprehensible, part of the omniscient adult world of pat solutions which just don't seem to apply to the special crises of the young (hence Dorothy's complaint that no one understands her). The use of close-ups here also serves a more functional purpose in terms of the plot; it foreshadows the reappearance of the three farmhands in the Oz sequence of the film.

Vidor's staging of "Over the Rainbow" with the camera following Dorothy likewise is done with the intent of getting the viewer to identify with her: the entire number consists of one long, unbroken shot which is interrupted only by an insert of the sun peering through the clouds (presumably emanating from that never-never land spoken of in the song). By the time this cut comes, the audience (by virtue of Judy Garland's mesmerizing rendition of the tune as well as the vicarious aspect of the direction—we stay with Dorothy throughout the entire number) has had its imagination aroused to such a terrific state that it is as eager as little Dorothy to escape to that wonderland "where troubles melt like lemon drops/so way above the chimney tops."

Judy Garland and Ray Bolger look on as Jack Haley does his routine.

Indeed, so great is our sympathy with Dorothy's plight at this point that the following scene—wherein Miss Gulch (Margaret Hamilton) demands that Dorothy surrender Toto to her for certain extermination—seems unusually uncomfortable. Miss Gulch is clearly an unreasonable woman (she stubbornly ignores Aunt Em's plea that Toto "could be tied up . . . he's really very gentle—with gentle people, that is") and is aptly branded "a wicked old witch" by Dorothy. Vidor effectively sums up the unbearable tension and conflict which Dorothy is experiencing at this moment by cutting to an extreme close-up of her anguished face as Toto is stuffed into Miss Gulch's basket (the rest of the scene has been very tactfully filmed, again, in one long take). Unable to bear the scene any longer, she rushes into her room and slams the door.

Our sense of identification with Dorothy reaches its apex during her hallucination after being struck by a flying window during the ensuing twister. After the house finally "lands" she cautiously gets up from her bed and looks around. After a minute or so, she comes to the door leading to the outside. The burst of blazing Technicolor which follows her opening of the door, combined with the forward tracking shot (again, from Dorothy's point of view) which carries us into Oz, permanently secures our interest in Dorothy's adventures for the remainder of the film. (Incidentally, and it is indeed surprising that not a single person who has spoken about *Oz* in the past has noticed this, the actual moment of transition from sepia to Technicolor is almost — but not quite — ruined, due to what appears to be a technical limitation in achieving the then-unprecedented effect. As soon as we get a shot of Dorothy spotting the door, there is a reel break. The next shot — the first in reel three — shows Dorothy at the door, which is no longer in sepia but in a reddish tint. Producer Mervyn LeRoy told Harmetz that each frame of the transition shot had to be hand-painted — which hints at what the ensuing footage will look like [the initial burst of Technicolor is still overwhelming, however]. Even with the immense technical resources which MGM had available in 1939, it was difficult, it appears, to effect a seamless transition from sepia to color in a single shot. The next feature to employ the technique, Fox's *The Blue Bird* (1940), used a simple cut to go from the black-and-white prologue to the story proper in color — as did the rather poor Abbott and Costello remake of *Jack and the Beanstalk* (1952).

By this point in the story, our suspension of disbelief has been achieved seemingly effortlessly by the careful (but unnoticed) attention which the writers and director have payed toward placing us firmly on Dorothy's side, thereby enabling us to view the remainder of the film from her perspective. The reason the entire Oz episode which follows intrigues us so completely is that it appeals to the basic imagination of the child in all of us. Its success in doing so derives from the fact that the whole adventure is treated as a *dream*, not a reality. According to Harmetz, this decision was made early on in the production stages: "Noel Langley's first treatment made it clear — as did the final movie — that Dorothy's adventures in Oz were only a dream." Harmetz feels that "as art, the movie is flawed by the

decision to void Dorothy's experience by making it into a dream."
Film professor Janet Juhnke's quote from a 19-year-old girl who
"left her Kansas home to make her way alone in New York City"
is even more specific:

> The ending is a total anticlimax. It states that this was all a
> dream, that fantasy is unreal and can only get you in trouble,
> and boring status quo existence is the right way to live . . .
> I hate the ending because fantasy *is* real, necessary, and
> because home is not always the best place to be.

Not so. The fact that Dorothy's trip to Oz is not treated as
a real experience (it *was*, however, in the Baum original) serves
several vital functions. First, it confirms the importance of the
establishment of perspective in the film's initial twenty minutes.
According to Harmetz, "All the scriptwriters felt it necessary to
have an audience relate to Dorothy in a real world before
transporting her to a fantasy one." There was always in the
screenwriters' minds the feeling that the two worlds should be
separate and distinct. Had Dorothy *really* traveled to Oz (and the
fact that she did not is confirmed from the very beginning and
emphasized throughout: a series of spiraling images after she is
struck by the window to indicate she's hallucinating; the wildly
exaggerated shot of the house plummeting to the ground; the fact
that Hunk, Hickory, Zeke, Prof. Marvel and Miss Gulch all have
Oz counterparts; Dorothy's statement to the Scarecrow and Tin
Man: "You know, it's funny, but I feel as if I'd known you all the
time," etc.), there would have been no need to spend more than
five minutes on her life in Kansas (and, indeed, Baum's description of Kansas took up no more than three short pages) — the fantastic elements of the picture would take over completely and
would only be intrinsically interesting.

The result would have been a lack of sympathy for Dorothy;
she would have seemed just another little girl in another routine
fairy tale (recall that what made Alice's adventures in wonderland
so spectacular was precisely the fact that they were ultimately
revealed to be creations of her imagination). There would have
been no need for farmhands with (semi)-distinct personalities

to parallel creatures in a fantasyland, nor would there need to have been a Miss Gulch to be reincarnated in the figure of a menacing witch. The phrase "semi-distinct" describes the farm-hands because, apart from an important line or two, they are given virtually nothing of significance to say—in fact, Hickory's declaration "Someday they're going to erect a statue to me in this town" seems very vague and at odds with the plight of his Oz counterpart, the Tin Man. Harmetz attributes this to the fact that "by the final script, a great deal of the conversation about the brainlessness of one farmhand who is applying to agricultural college and the heartlessness of the second was reduced to two or three sentences." But again, the important point to remember here is that it is Dorothy's *imagination* (her subconscious desire to escape her drab, unfeeling Kansas world) which enables her to create complex beings from the basically one-dimensional inhabitants of her prairie environment.

Perhaps the most fascinating example of this imagination principle involves Professor Marvel (Frank Morgan), the kindly but bogus clairvoyant whom Dorothy encounters on a lonely dirt road after running away from home. Before she even meets him, it is evident that she is intrigued by his vocation: she stands trans-fixed before the sign outside his caravan which proclaims "Pro-fessor Marvel—acclaimed by the Crowned Heads of Europe." We discover in no time, however, that he is only a charlatan: he unwittingly responds to Dorothy's query about his visiting the crowned heads with "Do you know any?" However, because Dorothy is so overcome with enthusiasm at the thought of escaping to faraway lands, she does not catch this slip of the tongue.

Marvel may not be a true magician, but he is a pretty fair judge of child psychology, managing to divine (after several un-successful guesses) that she is running away (again, Dorothy fails to grasp the truth: "Why, it's just as though you could read what was inside of me," she says, amazed). By the end of her encounter with him, she is convinced (from a glimpse into his "crystal ball") that Aunt Em is indeed sick with worry over her sudden disap-pearance. It is not surprising, therefore, that it is Marvel who has the greatest effect upon her subconscious: he turns up in Oz in no less than five different guises—most importantly, however, as the Wizard himself (there does exist a suspicion, however, that Frank Morgan's appearance in additional bit parts was a result of the producers' — or his agent's — desire to fatten up his role in the film — after all, his stint as the Wizard, though technically the starring role of the film, is considerably brief).

A factor worth noting here is the strange discrepancy between Dorothy's perception of Marvel as omniscient and the final revelation of the film that the Wizard is an ineffectual humbug. Although this vision of him is consistent in terms of character (he is revealed to be a fakir in both cases), it is somewhat incongruous if we consider that the entire film is taken from Dorothy's point of view. However, both Professor Marvel and the Wizard *do* share a desire to restore Dorothy safely to her home.

This scene in Marvel's caravan appeals to both the child and adult simultaneously: the child viewer (because he identifies so closely with Dorothy) is likely to overlook Marvel's tricking Dorothy (by telling her to close her eyes so as not to "disturb the spirits," taking a photo of her and Aunt Em out of her basket and inserting it into his crystal) and find comfort (along with her) in Marvel's "powers," while the adult audience will appreciate the ruse (it does not offend their sensibilities).

Because the dream aspect of the film's storyline is consistent with its adopting of a child's point-of-view, it also provides the means for a young viewer to separate fantasy from reality. It is important for any young person watching such sequences as Dorothy's imprisonment in the witch's castle to understand that such places as Oz exist *only* in dreams — after all, young people tend to take everything at face value. Had the screenwriters followed Baum's example, they would undoubtedly have succeeded in leaving many young viewers (who have been identifying with Dorothy for the entire length of the film) with the impression that they, too, could one day find themselves trapped in a horrible nightmare world similar to hers. This approach also satisfies the grownup crowd, who, of course, realize that such incidents are purely fictional (incidentally, the final credits list is in agreement with this realistic outlook: Morgan, Hamilton, Bolger, Lahr and Haley are billed under their Kansas names, with no mention of their Oz counterparts).

I disagree with Danny Peary's argument in his recent essay on *Oz* in *Cult Movies* that Dorothy should have remained in Oz since her adventures there were infinitely more exciting and happier than her drab existence in Kansas, where no one seemed to care about her, and where Miss Gulch was sure to come back to Toto as soon as she realized he'd escaped. Neither of these points is supported by the events in the film, first of all: Dorothy herself admits that although most of the *Oz* journey was "beautiful," she continually expressed a desire to leave that world and return home to those who loved her, for that is where she felt she belonged, no matter how much it would hurt to bid farewell to her Oz companions—who are, please remember, nothing but the counterparts of her three farmhands; if she had *truly* felt disagreeable towards them (for not hearing her out at the beginning), her unconscious would have blocked them out completely.

Furthermore, if Dorothy's relatives and friends on the farm were not concerned for her welfare, they certainly would not have ignored their chores to keep a vigil over her unconscious body—also, Professor Marvel had earlier caused Dorothy to rethink just how much Aunt Em really did care for her ("I had the measles once, and she stood by me every minute"); the point is the family's farm duties sometimes made them inaccessible for advice and counsel. Also, if Mr. Peary had indeed read Harmetz's book in its entirety (he recommends it for its production details), he would have noted that Noel Langley's "DO NOT MAKE CHANGES" script had the Professor Marvel character (actually called "Dr. Pink") assure Dorothy that he will not let the Sheriff take Toto away (granted, the omission of this line of dialogue was a careless oversight on the part of Florence Ryerson and Edgar Allan Woolf, however). More importantly, however, Peary's argument is disturbing from a conjectural standpoint. Most children these days tend to thrive on the macabre as opposed to the peaceful world of fairy tales (those of the Brothers Grimm notwithstanding): evidence the enormous—and depressing— kiddie turnouts at slice-and-dice horror flicks like *Friday the 13th.* So the majority of kids watching the Oz sequence would undoubtedly recall the Witch and her schemes most vividly of all—

making it absolutely necessary, as I said before, to emphasize that such events do not exist in the real world.

Peary's contention that the film's return to Kansas and its final emphasis on the "there's no place like home" theme weaken its artistic merits is nonsense: for most young people, there is *indeed* no place like home. Granted, the concept of having a character stray from his real-life surroundings and spend the rest of his life in a fantasyland is, at least superficially, a more daring concept from an artistic standpoint (and one which the film *Pufnstuf*, a direct variation on the *Oz* situation, failed to pull off, as we shall see), but, of course, is completely ludicrous from a practical one.

The point is that in order for an audience to believe in the fantastic elements of a story, the premise of that story must at least have some common theoretical grounds. The concept of Oz in itself is so totally farfetched that only a very young child could accept it as is; thus, as mentioned earlier, it becomes necessary to place the whole episode in an imaginary context in order to ensure its appeal to a mass audience — otherwise, the final result comes off as simply childish (which describes perfectly Frank Baum's *Oz* sequels, with their tales of four-headed monsters and so on — their political overtones notwithstanding).

The secret for the script's success in captivating both younger audiences and adults alike (who are, after all, children at heart) lies in the jokey attitude which the writers adopted in their explanations for the existence of fantastic things. According to Doug McClelland, "There was no heavy sense of coping with a classic, no pretentious effort to be other-worldly esoteric in the levity; the writers — and the improvisors — took a breezily contemporary, slangy, sometimes low-comedy approach that, like the other miracles of the production, has not dated — maybe even has gained in nostalgic charm with the years."

One of the main virtues of this approach is the frequent juxtaposition of the realistic with the fantastic in the same context. Perhaps the best example of this occurs in the Wizard's reassuring speech to Dorothy at the end of the film to the effect that he will be able to find a way to transport her back to Kansas. He tells her that he was once a balloonist with the Wonderland Carnival

Dorothy trapped in the witch's castle. Note Judy Garland's hair: a wig not used in the final version.

Company of Omaha, Nebraska (a state very similar to Dorothy's — another self-conscious recognition by the scenarists that this is all a dream), and that an accident caused him to lose control of the balloon one day. The next thing he knew, he had landed in Oz, where he was instantly proclaimed "the first Wizard Deluxe." "Times being what they were, I accepted the job," he says.

Here we have an overlapping of two different worlds — the "land of E. Pluribus Unum," as the Wizard describes the United States, and the fantasy world of Oz. The effect not only serves to make the fantasy more believable by the acknowledgment of its obvious absurdity (how could there exist such practical concerns as a depression in a place like Oz?), but more importantly assures the viewing audience (the young audience primarily) that Dorothy's return to Kansas is not far off. Indeed, Glinda's speech a few minutes later confirms that Dorothy has had the power to get back to Kansas all along. Throughout the film, this tongue-in-cheek attitude serves to relieve the impact of the frequent horrific elements — with one notable exception, which Harmetz is correct in labeling the most terrifying moment in the movie. It is the scene in the castle where the witch, after telling Dorothy she hasn't got long to live, abandons her temporarily in order to think up a "delicate" means of disposing with her.

Another advantage of the lighthearted approach of the scenarists is that all potential for sentimentality and sickly sweetness in the storyline is instantly nipped in the bud. Some examples: when Dorothy meets the Scarecrow, she is immediately caught off guard by the fact that he is able to talk. A typical (read: juvenile) approach to this scene would have been to have him utter lots of cutesy phrases such as "How now, brown cow?" in order to convince the audience of something of which they were already aware the first time they heard him open his mouth. Instead, the writers make the unusual situation into an opportunity for clever social commentary: when Dorothy asks the Scarecrow how he can talk if he hasn't got a brain, he *acknowledges* the incongruity of the situation and replies, "I don't know — but some people without brains do an awful lot of talking, don't they?" Incidentally, no one stops to ask the Tin Man how he is able to function without a heart, but his plight is treated in the same vein as the Scarecrow's: "When a man's an empty kettle/ He should be on his metal/And yet I'm torn apart." Of course, the Cowardly Lion's name is itself an amusing paradox. There is potential slushiness in the moment when Dorothy breaks into tears at the thought of never getting home after the Emerald City guard tells her the Wizard will not see her. However, the scene is rescued just in time by having the guard (unseen by the foursome) reappear at the gate and observe the situation. After listening to Dorothy's lament, he is himself moved to tears, and finally relents with: "All right, all right. I'll get you in to see the Wizard somehow. I had an Aunt Em myself once." The wittiness of this last line of dialogue, combined with the hysterical slobberings of the guard (played by the incomparable Frank Morgan), result in eliciting not a wince but a hearty chuckle from the viewer.

Judy Garland sings the immortal "Over the Rainbow."

The most memorably written (and performed) scene (in a film full of memorable scenes) remains the one in which the Wizard hands out the gifts to Dorothy and her three friends. The aforementioned technique of the writers is here put to perfection: we get the implication that the Scarecrow, Tin Man and Cowardly Lion have shown throughout the course of the film that they already possess the qualities they have been seeking without having it elaborately spelled out for us. The Wizard simply responds to the Scarecrow's request with "Why, anybody can have a brain. That's a very mediocre commodity"—and, pressed by the Scarecrow as to what the "Ph. D." in his "honorary degree" stands for, he mumbles off the top of his head: "Doctor of Thinkology" (i.e., it doesn't make any difference). And the potential for stickiness in the cases of Dorothy and the Tin Man is cleverly avoided as well. The Wizard's advice to the latter ("Remember, my sentimental friend, that a heart is not judged by how much *you* love, but by how much you are loved by others") is relieved of all its inherent sentimental overtones by his giving the Woodman a *metal* heart on a chain (telling him, "Hearts will never be practical until they can be made unbreakable") and by the recipient's response: "Look—it ticks!" As for Dorothy's situation, her despairing "I don't think there's anything in that little black bag for me" (in other words, it looks like I'll never get home now) is happily relieved when the Wizard turns out to be, incredibly, another fugitive from the Midwestern United States!

What is most incredible about *Oz* is that aspects of the Baum book which were changed out of practical necessity in the transition to the screen and which would at first sight appear to be a detriment to the film's success are magically transformed into assets. According to Harmetz,

> What is lost in the translation from book to movie is *innocence*. Internal evidence within the fourteen books that L. Frank Baum wrote about *Oz* suggests that Dorothy was five or six years old at the time of her first visit. Sixteen-year-old Judy Garland might be carefully corseted and dressed in gingham to appear twelve, but she could never have made believable the simple, uncritical acceptance of the very young child who was Dorothy in the book. Innocence had been given its death blow, of course, by the fact that the Scarecrow, Tin Woodman and Cowardly Lion were played by three actors trained in burlesque and vaudeville. Haley, Bolger and Bert Lahr created their characters out of their vaudeville personalities.

Now, one might think at first glance that using actors of such incongruous (for a children's story) backgrounds would result in a coarsening of the essential innocence of the tale, an unnecessary undercurrent of nastiness or cruelty. However, the fact that Bolger, Haley and Lahr created their characters out of their vaudeville personalities not only serves to make the atmosphere of the film *more* gay and carefree, but at the same time provides the scenarists with an opportunity for clever puns which enhance the gentle humor of the situations while never becoming condescending to the children in the audience. As Harmetz says, Bolger's "good-natured, almost lazy physical grace that had caused Walter Winchell to label him 'America's Soft-Shoe Man' dominated his Scarecrow"—and it is precisely that quality which lifts his first meeting with Dorothy out of the realm of the mundane into the realm of the unforgettable. Again, Dorothy's joyous expression of surprise at the Scarecrow's (i.e.,

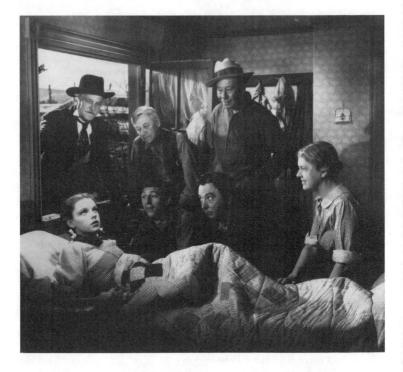

Dorothy awakens to discover it was all a dream. Frank Morgan, Clara Blandick, Charley Grapewin, Ray Bolger, Jack Haley and Bert Lahr look on.

Bolger's) incredible agility as he dances to "If I Only Had a Brain" serves — since we are watching the film through her eyes — as a mirror for our own feelings of exhilaration.

The same can be said for Haley's soft-shoe (in a tin costume yet). Since, as he said, "My character in show business was always a Milquetoast who was filled with fear . . . the Tin Woodman was a very easy part." Likewise for Lahr, who "had started out as a Dutch comedian in burlesque — a dialect comedian, the most physical and unsophisticated type of comedy. His Cowardly Lion was the summation of his early career, allowing him to give full vent to the bow-wow braggadocio of his personality." It is Lahr for whom many of the funniest lines in the film were written — mostly by Yip Harburg, who penned the lyrics to the film's songs. Since, as Harmetz points out, Harburg and Harold

Arlen (who wrote the music) had worked for Lahr before, "each of the Cowardly Lion's songs was a specific comment on his stage personality, incorporating mannerisms he had already made famous on Broadway." Lahr is given *two* numbers—the second, "If I Were King of the Forest," a standout—whereas Bolger and Haley have one apiece. This is what caused several critics reviewing the film back in 1939 to state that it was Lahr who ultimately stole the show. The odds do seem to be in his favor at certain points, such as his first meeting with Dorothy, the Scarecrow and the Tin Man. Here he has a barrage of one-liners: "How long you stay fresh in that can?" he asks the Tin Man. He likewise calls the Scarecrow a "lopsided bag of hay." However, from today's standpoint any talk of upstaging would practically be sacrilegious.

As for Judy Garland's being too old for the role of Dorothy, a simple comparison with 10-year-old Fairuza Balk's amateurish interpretation of her in 1985's *Return to Oz* is proof enough that Garland's natural talents as an actress, fostered by her previous training (she appeared in seven features prior to *Oz*, whereas Balk's stint as Dorothy marked her screen debut) is what lends maturity to her interpretation, preventing her from ever overdoing it with ga-ga eyes and "Oh, my!" expressions, while at the same time allowing a sense of childlike wonder to remain ever-present in her characterization (whatever the technical quibbles about her age—she was 16 at the time, whereas Baum's Dorothy was 12—Garland certainly doesn't *look* a day over 15). Even Harmetz, who objects to the age discrepancy, concedes that Garland displayed "absolute sincerity . . . it is her obvious belief in what is happening to her that keeps the film credible."

Harmetz credits most of the success of Garland's performance to director Victor Fleming. Fleming at first glance would not seem to conform to producer Mervyn LeRoy's idea of a director "with the mind of a child": Fleming in real life was a roughneck and a motorcycle rider whose previous pictures, such as MGM's *Test Pilot* (1938) and *Captains Courageous* (1937), had depicted "a world of rough men, rough skies, rough seas." However, as McClelland points out, "Fleming had (also) evidenced a sensitive touch with youngsters in such films as *Captains*

Courageous with Freddie Bartholomew." According to John Lee
Mahin, as quoted by Harmetz, "I think [Vic took on the job] for
Missy and Sally [his two daughters]. I was with him on the set and
I could see his whole love for them poured into the picture."
Nevertheless, he kept his actors firmly in line at all times. Bolger:
"He was like an army officer. He stood for no foolishness."
Hamilton: "He could be very sarcastic. And he did have one dilly
of a temper."

So, based on this information (and the light touch of fantasy
evidenced in the final film) it would seem that the ideal director
for a children's picture is one who can be both gentle and
strict—even slightly sadistic at times—a rare combination, indeed. We will see that future efforts in this genre bear out this
contention. The most successful efforts are those in which the
director understands and loves children (Ken Hughes on *Chitty
Chitty Bang Bang* and Mel Stuart on *Willy Wonka* are two of the
best examples of this type), but who never allow themselves to
become simply "yes-men," carrying out the wishes of others
without imparting many ideas of their own (i.e., Charles Vidor on
Hans Christian Andersen, Richard Fleischer on *Dr. Dolittle* and
others). There is never for a moment in *Oz* evidence of the strain-
ing to achieve a goody-goody "kiddie" atmosphere of sweetness
and light which would prove the downfall of such later efforts as
Disney's *Babes in Toyland* (1961, Jack Donohue). Even the potential saccharine quality of such a character as Glinda is overcome
by the "slightly fey quality" of actress Billie Burke, which,
Harmetz says, "played well against the acidulous menace of
Margaret Hamilton ... [Burke lightened] the menace by
treating it as an incomprehensible annoyance." For example,
after the Witch departs from Munchkinland in a burst of smoke
and fire, Burke waves her arms and exclaims, "What a smell of
sulphur!" It is interesting to note that Burke and Hamilton are actually on screen for only about *ten minutes* apiece! It is a credit
to their talents that they were able to leave such an indelible
mark on audiences—certainly the threat of the Witch pervades
even the most serene moments of the story, and the audience is
likewise always aware that, however serious the menace of the
Witch becomes, Glinda the Good is never far behind.

"If I Only Had a Brain": Ray Bolger as the Scarecrow.

In addition to his work with the actors, the other noteworthy contribution of director Fleming is his (and editor Blanche Sewell's — they worked on the picture at night after Fleming's daily work on *Gone with the Wind* had ended) success in maintaining a consistency of tempo — no small feat in a film which had no fewer than five different screenwriters. Indeed, once one is familiar with the story, the film seems to zip by. Doug McClelland says that Bolger's role "should have allowed more of his specialty, comic dancing" — well, in fact, it originally *did:* additional footage (about five minutes in length) of Bolger's dance routine from "If I Only Had a Brain" was discovered recently in the MGM vaults and displayed in the 1985 theatrical release *That's Dancing.* Narrator Sammy Davis, Jr.'s, remark in that film to the effect that "no one quite knows why that lovely and charming little number was deleted from the final print of *The Wizard of Oz*" seems somewhat naive if one looks carefully at the picture. It is obvious that Fleming wanted to keep the introductory numbers of the Scarecrow, Tin Man and Lion on a par in terms of screen time so that there would be no evidence of favoritism — and so the pace of the film would not be slowed down (however, Bolger's number does seem to end rather abruptly, even to the viewer unfamiliar with the rediscovered footage, and its omission is particularly unjust when one realizes that Haley has a short dance routine which follows his song).

Fleming also deleted "The Jitterbug" and the "Renovation Sequence" which preceded the foursome's return to the Wizard at the end — the former because it would date the picture, the latter because it seemed a lengthy and unnecessary diversion from the main storyline — although he left in Lahr's "If I Were King of the Forest." As mentioned before, the inclusion of this last number left several critics with the impression that Lahr's character overshadowed the others. From today's standpoint, however, *any* "lost" footage from this movie treasure is eagerly welcomed by audiences — in fact, some New York revival houses reportedly screen on occasion a print of *Oz* with "The Jitterbug" included, to the delight of thousands of fans of the picture who do not feel the number dates it in the least — after all, there are enough other characteristics (the garish Technicolor, for one) which already brand the film as a remnant of the bygone Studio Era of the '30s and '40s (and it is certainly possible that all "lost" footage will be restored for *Oz*'s 50th anniversary).

Jack Haley told Harmetz that "There was no acting (in the film). It was all movement. We were running all the time. We were always afraid. We had three lines and then we were off to see the Wizard. We were running all over the joint — putting out fires, chopping down doors, cutting down the rope that held the witch's chandelier. The only scenes that had any acting value were in black-and-white when Judy met Frank Morgan and he looked in his crystal ball." This statement is actually a tribute to Fleming's success as a director: the film is so briskly paced in terms of the action that one never has time to *notice* that the actors are acting. There are, in point of fact, quite a number of affecting scenes — among them Dorothy's initial meetings with her three friends and their explanations of their plights; the moment after Dorothy has been abducted where the Scarecrow, Tin Man and Lion decide that it is their duty to save her from the Witch's clutches; and her final goodbyes to them (especially her whispering to the Scarecrow, "I think I'll miss you most of all").

It is the cumulative effect of all the performances with which one comes away from the film — and which makes it so endearing to all who see it.

The accomplishments of Fleming, the performers, set designers and the other technicians appear all the more remarkable when one considers that most of the film was shot in color (and, as noted before, decidedly garish-looking color at that). Color is notorious for exposing the intricacies of all aspects of a production — from camera movement to decor and mattes. In the case of *Oz*, this is unfortunately true in the case of the Munchkinland sets. Not surprisingly, it is the sepia mattes (the Kansas landscapes, the shot of the sun peering through the clouds, the twister) which go by unnoticed. Oddly enough, Harmetz picks as one of the few moments in the film where art is evident the first shot of Emerald City seen from the Poppy Field — this is actually one of the most artificial, *un*believable moments in the film. Emerald City itself, however, is a thoroughly convincing set — actually, this is a contradiction in terms, since a good set is like a good toupee: it is only successful if it is not noticed as such.

Orson Welles always used to say that people seem to give better performances in black-and-white films, since in black-and-white, the focus is on faces rather than scenery. In light of this, the actors deserve even more credit than either I or the others who have written about the film in the past have given them. Their task was twofold: not only were they required to engage our interest throughout, but they had to do so in the face of some eye-popping set decorations which constantly threatened to divert the viewer's attention away from the main action. They also had to endure the agony of the 1000-candle lights which the 3-strip Technicolor process employed by the studio necessitated (particularly burdensome for Haley, Hamilton, Bolger and Lahr).

Also indispensable to the film's success (in addition to the songs, which are inspired, to say the least) is the filmmakers' method of shooting the musical numbers — using unbroken long takes in order to emphasize the action within the frame and give the performers an opportunity to do an entire dance or song in its entirety. This has always proven to be the best way to shoot numbers; it is the method which the great directors and choreographers (Lubitsch, Mamoulian, Astaire, Sandrich, Minnelli and Kelly) employed throughout their careers.

In the end, the continuing popularity of *The Wizard of Oz* (and Harmetz is correct in stating that it is repeated each year "because it has become a part of American culture") stems from a few simple facts. First, there was real magic going on behind and in front of the camera — that wonderful, intangible quality which cannot be purchased with a large budget (as so many later efforts in this genre would prove) — although this is not to say that *Oz* was not an extraordinarily expensive production for its time, coming in at $2,777,000, the equivalent of $40 million by today's standards — but which results from the tireless efforts of true professionals who are dedicated to their craft (and this term, better than any other, typifies the studio era of moviemaking).

Secondly, there was no attempt on the part of the filmmakers to deal with social issues which were beyond the boundaries of a simple fairy story. As Ray Bolger put it, "The philosophy of *Oz* is man's search for basic human needs — a heart, brains, courage. And that, chum, will never be old hat."

Since the publication of Harmetz's and McClelland's books, nearly all of the remaining persons associated with *Oz* have, sadly, passed on: George Cukor, Jack Haley, Margaret Hamilton, E.Y. Harburg, Harold Arlen, Noel Langley, King Vidor, and, most recently, the last surviving cast member, Ray Bolger, producer Mervyn LeRoy and cinematographer Harold Rosson (only choreographer Bobby Connolly survives). The thought that virtually all of the *Oz* cast and crew are gone makes watching the film today, nearly a half century after its release, a bittersweet experience; like its great contemporary, *Gone with the Wind, Oz* remains a remnant of a bygone era — bygone, but hardly forgotten: Jack Haley spoke for most of the actors and technical personnel who were involved with the production when he said, "The other pictures I made — who [will remember them]? But when I'm dead and gone, *The Wizard of Oz* will be forever." Amen.

Hans Christian Andersen

A Samuel Goldwyn Presentation, distributed by RKO Radio Pictures, 1952. *Producer* Samuel Goldwyn. *Director* Charles Vidor. *Screenplay* Moss Hart, *based on a story by* Myles Connolly. *Words and Music* Frank Loesser. *Director of Photography* Harry Stradling, A.S.C. *Choreography* Roland Petit. *Musical Director* Walter Scharf. *Art Directors* Richard Day and Clave. *Editor* Daniel Mandell, A.C.E. *Ballet Costumes designed by* Clave, *executed by* Madame Karinska. *Other Costumes* Mary Wills. *Set Decorations* Howard Bristol. *Special Photographic Effects* Clarence Slifer. *Technicolor Color Consultant* Richard Mueller. *Orchestrations* Jerome Moross. *Makeup* Del Armstrong. *Hair Stylist* Helen Turpin. *Sound Recorder* Fred Lau. Western Electric Recording. Technicolor. Running Time: 112 minutes.

Cast Danny Kaye (Hans Christian Andersen), Farley Granger (Niels), Jeanmaire (Doro), Joey Walsh (Peter), Philip Tonge (Otto), Erik Bruhn (The Hussar), Roland Petit (The Prince in "The Little Mermaid" Ballet), John Brown (Schoolmaster), John Qualen (Burgomaster), Jeanne Lafayette (Celine), Robert Malcom (Stage Doorman), George Chandler (Farmer), Fred Kesley (First Gendarme), Gil Perkins (Second Gendarme), Peter Votrian (Lars).

Songs "The King's New Clothes," "Inchworm," "I'm Hans Christian Andersen," "Wonderful Copenhagen," "Thumbelina," "The Ugly Duckling," "Anywhere I Wander," "No Two People" words and music by Frank Loesser.

American cinema in the 1940s, preoccupied as it was with war and its consequences, *film noir,* and socially critical subjects which demanded a documentary realism, was hardly the place for the lighthearted escapism of a children's musical. Indeed, it was not until 1951 that a new effort in the genre was to emerge — although the germ of inspiration had already been brewing in the mind of mogul Samuel Goldwyn for some time. He had this to say in a *New York Times* article preceding the release of *Hans Christian Andersen* in 1952:

> This picture is the culmination of something I have dreamed about during waking as well as sleeping—and sleepless—hours since the idea of a Hans Christian Andersen picture first caught my imagination back in 1936 . . . from that first moment sixteen years ago I have always visualized it as something completely different from anything which had ever been done in pictures. I suppose that is why it took all those years of writing and rewriting—some thirty-eight scripts in all—before Moss Hart was finally able to capture the spirit of Hans Christian Andersen as I had envisioned it. . . . I wanted to put on the screen . . . the essence of Hans Christian Andersen as a writer—[his ability] to take readers into a world of imagination, peopled with mermaids and princesses and snow queens and foolish emperors and wise children and ugly ducklings who turned into beautiful swans.

It was perhaps not terribly surprising that Goldwyn, whose studio had been responsible for much of the lighter fare during the oppressive past decade—mainly a handful of Danny Kaye and Bob Hope farces—would be the one to resurrect the children's film. Unfortunately, as one of his biographers, Arthur Marx, has pointed out, the result was not to be much better than those mediocre color spectaculars—the comedies *Up in Arms* (1944), *The Princess and the Pirate* (1944), *The Secret Life of Walter Mitty* (1947) and the musical *A Song Is Born* (1948) among them—which had assured healthy profits for Samuel Goldwyn Productions during the troubled war years. Many of the problems with the final feature can be traced directly to the above statements by the producer; they alone are ample evidence for refuting Michael Freedland's assertion in his *Secret Life of Danny Kaye* to the effect that "Goldwyn was not the legendary Hollywood mogul with abysmal taste who was only interested in making money, not works of art."

It has become an almost universal contention over the years that the only motion pictures produced by Goldwyn with any valid claims to fame as works of art are the eight features directed between 1935 and 1947 by one man, William Wyler, and photographed by another, Gregg Toland, the best of the lot being 1946's *The Best Years of Our Lives*. Incredibly enough, Wyler was Goldwyn's first choice to direct *Andersen*, with Gary Cooper — who had worked with Wyler in 1940's *The Westerner* — as star! Although both were indisputably more talented than Charles Vidor and Danny Kaye, who were finally chosen, it is certain that the result would still have been disastrous; Wyler was in fact to direct his one and only musical, *Funny Girl*, 16 years later with two of the important creative personnel who worked on *Andersen*, cinematographer Harry Stradling and musical conductor Walter Scharf, aboard, though with only middling success; but certainly *Funny Girl* exists on a higher aesthetic plane than *Andersen*.

Goldwyn's "talent," if it may indeed be described as such, consisted solely of his knack for hiring the best possible creative personnel for each individual production (Walter Scharf, who scored several Goldwyn films, including *Andersen*, attests to this also). Otto Preminger, who directed Goldwyn's last production, the disastrous *Porgy and Bess* (1959), once said of him: "He was not a producer like David Selznick or Zanuck, who really inspired people, and contributed something. He only knew always to buy the best." (Pratley, *The Cinema of Otto Preminger*, p. 126). As we shall see in the case of *Hans Christian Andersen*, Goldwyn more often than not made the wrong choices precisely because he was far more capable of assessing the potential box-office value of certain "name" collaborators than of judging their artistic qualifications for this particular project.

As Goldwyn points out in the first sentence of his statement to the American public, a film about the famous Danish storyteller had been a dream of his for more than a decade. It no doubt came as a shock to many to hear this man who had been described by Preminger (and countless others) as "cold-blooded" and "very egotistical, with an awful way of testing people to see if they really knew their business, even when they had proved themselves," suddenly speaking wistfully about snow queens and foolish emperors and little mermaids. Indeed, the very personal nature of this project seems to have brought to the fore for the first time a formerly repressed aspect of the man's nature (namely a rather childish naivete) and as a result seems to have clouded his usually keen judgment in choosing the right people for the right positions.

Although Goldwyn at 71 still retained much of the fire and brimstone of his younger self, it was more than clear that his interest in and ability for producing were waning: he would turn out only two more features after *Hans*, both musicals and both artistic failures: *Guys and Dolls* (1955: Marlon Brando and Jean Simmons singing!) and, as just mentioned, *Porgy and Bess*—of which the Gershwin estate is so ashamed that they acquired the rights to it several years ago to prevent its being screened anywhere.

What is most remarkable about *Hans Christian Andersen* is how Goldwyn could have so fatally compromised a project that was perhaps more important to him than even *Best Years*, which had won him both an Oscar for Best Picture and the Irving Thalberg award back in 1947.

It might be argued that since Goldwyn knew he would be getting out of the business in a short time, and since the concept was still too close to his heart for him to abandon it, he was willing to settle for whatever was available in the way of creative talent in 1951, when production began. But that is not the case. As he himself points out, the script went through some 38 rewrites before he settled on the final one by Moss Hart—and according to Arthur Marx, Goldwyn based his decision to make the film solely on his obtaining that *particular* script.

In addition, with the exception of stars Danny Kaye and Farley Granger, none of the prominent players or production artists were contracted to Goldwyn Studios, but were handpicked by Goldwyn for various reasons known only to him. In view of the final product, the kindest (or at least the most accurate) phrase for describing *Hans Christian Andersen* would seem to be "an old man's conceit"—the latter word having been used by Pauline Kael in her review (*5001 Nights*, p. 240).

The problems with *Andersen* can be traced directly back to those opening remarks of Goldwyn. Here are his feelings as to why Andersen the writer would make an interesting subject for a film:

> Underneath all his tales I found a very basic philosophy — if
> I can use such a pretentious word for a very simple approach
> to life — of faith and trust in the capacity of everyone to get
> the most out of life if only he utilizes the powers within him.
> The picture does not paint any moral — heaven forbid — but
> the happy-go-lucky Andersen of the picture does seem to say
> that if you use your imagination, if you give your spirit free
> play, if you don't try to be someone else but are content to be
> true to yourself, you will find joy, happiness and beauty all
> around you.

Already there are hints as to the wishy-washy approach to the
character of Andersen which Moss Hart's script would eventually
take. Goldwyn does not mention, of course, that he and Hart had
made the decision to confine the scope of their picture to "a fairy
tale about that great spinner of fairy tales" (as the prologue to the
film states) to ease the minds of those who were expecting a biography of the man. And indeed the imminent release of the picture was met with pressure from the Danish government, which
threatened to make a formal protest against the film because, according to Marx, having an American play Andersen "was insulting to his memory." (That the Danes were just as quickly
placated by the worldwide success of Frank Loesser's song
"Wonderful Copenhagen," which started a tourist boom in the
famous city, is a sad indication of just exactly where their priori-
ties lay when it came to artistic integrity, but that is another
matter.)

What is perhaps the biggest surprise of all is that a screen
biography of Andersen had most likely *never* been foremost in
Goldwyn's mind: all of the scripts he had commissioned over the
previous 16 years were based on a single source, a novella (or
short story) called *The Story of Hans Christian Andersen* by
children's book author Myles Connolly. Unfortunately, according to Connolly's daughter, there are no extant copies of the
story, as it was written directly for Goldwyn and became the
property of Goldwyn Studios (for that reason it was never
published in a collection). Since neither Sam Goldwyn, Jr., nor
Kitty Carlisle, Hart's widow, knows anything of its whereabouts
either, it is reasonable to assume the source is gone forever.

Peter (Joey Walsh) attempts to persuade Hans (Danny Kaye) to go to Copenhagen.

It is probably a safe guess, however, that Connolly's story had as little to do with Andersen's life as Hart's script (or those of any of the other rejected screenwriters, for that matter) does—and that none of the 38 overlooked scripts could have been so drastically different in concept from Hart's, since, after all, they were all faithfully derived from a source that was most likely no longer than 50 pages. The fact that the final version written by Hart is so disappointing (and more on that score presently) makes Goldwyn's postponing the project for so long—along with his decision to make the film in the first place—particularly suspect.

His published explanation for undertaking the venture is about as far from a concrete conception of the man, or of his work, or of the artistic potentials of such a film, as one could imagine—in fact, Goldwyn makes the pic sound no different from a run-of-the-mill World War II escapist musical (or musical comedy):

> I wanted to put on the screen something which would take the people who saw it completely away from the cares and routines of daily life. After years of war—both "hot" and "cold"—it seemed to me that people would welcome an opportunity to get away from the realities of the middle of the twentieth century into a special world of one's own making.

Before becoming too specific about the film's flaws, however, it would probably be a good idea to give a plot summary. In the little town of Odense, Denmark, in 1830, Hans Christian Andersen (Danny Kaye) is the village cobbler and a spinner of tall tales. His stories are so popular with the local children that they play hookey from school to hear them. Every time Hans feels like telling one, he signals his desire by flying his kite.

Hans's young apprentice, Peter (Joey Walsh), is constantly warning him of the trouble he will eventually incur from the city council for keeping the children from their studies. One day the schoolmaster of the village (John Brown) decides he has had enough, and delivers an ultimatum to the council: either Hans Christian Andersen or he must go. The townspeople, who also feel that Hans is filling their youngsters' heads with nonsensical "lessons" ("I asked my little girl what time it was. She told me the big hand and the little hand weren't speaking, and that they wouldn't make up until they met at 12 o'clock, and no one would be able to tell the time until then!" exclaims one man), back up the schoolmaster's statements, and so the Burgomaster (John Qualen) reluctantly agrees to speak to Hans that evening.

To spare Hans the ignominy of being banished from the town, Peter talks him into leaving voluntarily. He then sets out in pursuit of Hans, catching up with him the next day. Together they make their way to the magic city of Copenhagen.

Immediately upon arrival, Hans decides to set up his cobbler's shop in the heart of the Great Square. He climbs up on the base of a huge equestrian statue to attract trade—and two policemen promptly arrest him for "disrespect to the King's statue." They also try to grab Peter but he escapes down the street.

Looking for a safe hiding place, Peter darts into a doorway at the end of an alley. It turns out to be the stage entrance to the Royal Theater. As he crouches in a dark corner, he overhears two men arguing. One man, Otto (Philip Tongue), is asking the other, the Ballet Director, Niels (Farley Granger), where, on a holiday, he will be able to find a cobbler. Peter emerges from the shadows and tells Otto that he knows where a cobbler sits this very minute — but in order to secure his services he will have to use a little influence with the police.

Hans is soon released from jail and placed in the custody of the Royal Danish Ballet. He is then commissioned to make a special pair of slippers for the Ballerina, Doro (Jeanmaire). All she wants is the impossible — shoes that will walk on air. But Hans, falling in love with her at first sight, promises that she shall have them.

Hans is scornful of the harsh treatment which Doro receives from Niels. Unbeknownst to him, however, the two of them are actually happily married — their squabbles are purely of a professional nature, with one always dreaming up some way of tormenting the other.

The following noon, between rehearsals, Doro confesses to Niels that there was nothing wrong with her shoes. It was just that she knew the unreasonable demand for a new pair on a holiday would get his goat. Niels immediately spits back. This starts a fight, which culminates with the Ballerina hauling off and slapping her husband and he promptly slapping her back — just as Hans is arriving with the new pair of shoes. He is shocked when the stage manager, who prevents him from barging in on the rehearsal, informs him that the two are in fact husband and wife.

That night Hans writes a letter to Doro. It is a love letter, but he disguises it in the form of a fairy tale. It concerns a mermaid who gradually comes to realize that she has sought love from the wrong man. Peter tries to convince Hans that he does not know the truth about them (he has been eavesdropping on their intimate conversation over lunch), but Hans ignores him: "You're a child, you don't understand."

In the middle of the night Peter gets up to read the letter. Hans stirs in his sleep and Peter jumps, guiltily hiding the letter behind his back. A sudden breeze blows the paper out of his hand. It sails down the alley and finally disappears through an open window of the theater. He spies it on a ledge but in trying to retrieve it he wakens the doorman, who takes the letter to the Ballerina. Under questioning by Niels, Peter admits that Hans wrote it. The Ballerina glances at it and concludes that the cobbler has written her a ballet.

Back in their room Peter tells Hans that the Ballerina has his letter. He sees the fact that "the wind took it to her" as "an omen," and wants to rush to her and tell her of his great love for her. Peter tries to spare him the humiliation of learning the truth, but Hans refuses to listen. He rushes to the theater only to find that the ballet has left town on its annual tour.

Hans remains behind in Copenhagen and sets up shop near the river. He is soon up to his old tricks of telling stories to children in the park. One day he meets a little boy whose bald head is a target for the other children's teasing. He makes up the story of "The Ugly Duckling" who discovered that he was actually a swan, which cheers up the youngster. The boy's father, it turns out, is a newspaper publisher, and offers to repay Hans for his good deed by printing the story in the *Copenhagen Weekly Gazette*. He offers to do the same for any future tales Hans might come up with. Hans has a new career as a writer.

Meanwhile, the ballet returns from its tour. On opening night the Ballerina plans to dance Hans' ballet, "The Little Mermaid." Peter tries to dissuade Hans from attending, insisting that he is "making up a story about Doro and Niels in his head just like he does about everything else. Only this time it's about *them*, not clocks and flowers and stars. She'll laugh at you, Hans." Hans accuses Peter of lying to him and suggests that perhaps they should part company altogether. Hans departs for the theater alone.

When Hans arrives at the theater with a present for the Ballerina, a new pair of slippers, Niels refuses to let him see her. When Hans persists, Niels locks him in the prop broom closet, and Hans misses the thrill of seeing his story brought to life by the dance. But he can hear the orchestra. As the music swells, Hans envisions the ballet as a declaration of his love which, in his mind, the Ballerina returns. He falls blissfully asleep.

The next morning, in her apartment, the Ballerina wonders why Hans hadn't attended the opening. Niels confesses he locked the cobbler up. Very upset, Doro sends her maid to fetch Hans. She tries to apologize for her husband's action, but Hans tells her there's no need. When she tells him she felt something "sad and tender" when dancing the ballet that she cannot quite put her finger on, Hans offers an explanation: "I think it was your answer. I let my heart speak to you with the story and last night you answered me with yours."

It suddenly dawns on the Ballerina that Hans is in love with her. She asked him how he happened to write the story. "How else could a cobbler speak to you?" he replies. "How else could I tell you how unhappy I knew you were with your husband?" Doro is afraid to tell Hans the truth for fear of hurting him. Just then Niels bursts into the room with an extravagant piece of jewelry for his wife. They kiss passionately. As if that weren't embarrassing enough for Hans, Niels reveals that Doro was laughing about his locking Hans in the closet "even under the covers." Before Hans leaves, Niels asks him if he has any other stories which the ballet company can use. "No, I'm afraid that one was just a fluke. I won't be writing any more stories," he replies sadly. Then, holding out the new shoes which he has brought the Ballerina, he declares, "I guess it's all right to deliver these now. Some shoes from the cobbler."

Hans is next seen returning to Odense. On the way he catches up with Peter, and tells him that he is through with storytelling. But Peter is certain that he will continue to tell them. "Why do you keep saying that?" Hans asks. "Why? Because you're Hans Christian Andersen, that's why." And Peter is right, for Hans becomes a celebrity to the people of Odense. Now everyone turns out to hear his stories—even the schoolmaster.

According to Arthur Marx, "If anyone had the qualifications to write the story of Hans Christian Andersen, it should have been Moss Hart." He cites Hart's coauthoring of the Pulitzer Prize–winning *You Can't Take It with You* and Hart's own *Lady in the Dark* as sufficient credentials. Although Hart's talents as a writer need no qualification at this late date, nothing in his past, either in his works for the stage or his handful of screenplays, would lead anyone (except Goldwyn) to believe that he would be the right man to pen what is basically a children's tale.

Moss Hart's work prior to *Andersen* consisted of sophisticated drawing-room comedies like *The Man Who Came to Dinner*, screwball farces like *You Can't Take It with You* and *George Washington Slept Here*, and scathing satires like *Once in a Lifetime*, all co-written with George S. Kaufman and all eventually made into films both good and mediocre. Up to 1951 he had written three screenplays, the only one of which worth mentioning (and just barely at that) is 1947's then-controversial but now rather bland liberal melodrama *Gentleman's Agreement*, from the Laura Z. Hobson novel.

Andersen was Hart's first work to be written directly for the screen. The only reasonable explanation I can offer for his agreeing to take on the project is that he was probably anxious to do another film at that time, as his successful partnership with Kaufman had ended, and he hadn't exactly been working steadily over the previous three or four years. No doubt the chance to tackle formerly unexplored subject matter stimulated his imagination also (this quality is probably what caused Goldwyn to seek him out in the first place, although Hart hadn't exactly earned a reputation for astounding versatility—Goldwyn was probably simply impressed with his track record), but more likely it was Goldwyn's offer of a large salary that excited him.

The script which Hart completed for Goldwyn, as has been stated by others, does not have much to do with Andersen the man *or* with Andersen the writer. What indeed is the point of calling a picture *Hans Christian Andersen*—a title which would lead any reasonable person to expect a biography—and then instead delivering a product which is neither a credible reflection of the subject's life nor even a terribly interesting takeoff on that life story—in short, a "pseudo-whimsical monstrosity" (Pauline Kael)? The film finally amounts to little more than a fabricated conceit which makes perhaps the most larger-than-life figure in the history of children's literature out to be, quite simply, "a simpleton bordering on active idiocy" (Kael again).

To the script's credit (though this undoubtedly has more to

do with Connolly's original story than with any insight on the part of Hart or Goldwyn) it does occasionally touch upon aspects of Andersen's life, in particular with the movie Andersen's failure to find love with the Ballerina. It is a well-known fact that during the course of his lifetime the real Andersen was painfully smitten with three women of various backgrounds foreign to his, and that none of the three ever returned his affections (of course, the fact that in the film the Ballerina is already married does not help matters much, but there is still the hint that she could never see him as anything but an amiable country bumpkin anyway). The fame which Andersen received for his writings helped ease his loneliness, and this can be perceived in the film's brief closing scene wherein Hans — most likely still a bachelor — is seen many years after his visit to Copenhagen happily entertaining a new generation of children with his tales.

Despite a final montage of Andersen storybook covers meant to illustrate the scope of the man's work, there is little indication from the script that the man whom Danny Kaye portrays could have even mastered the craft of fixing shoes (he expresses disappointment at the sloppy job his apprentice Peter has done on one pair at the beginning), let alone have created magical tales that captured the hearts of millions. As *New York Times* critic Bosley Crowther put it, "although Kaye's Andersen is supposed to be a fellow with a fantastic gift of gab and a hypnotic way with children, he has little to say of interest — except in song."

Crowther's description of the character as "a sort of amiable village dunce" is right on target — just sample the following dialogue from a scene (cut from the picture for years but restored in 1984) in which Andersen speaks to a stray dog on the road to Copenhagen:

> You want to know something, my friend? I'm a little scared. Copenhagen is a very big place. Still, what can happen, huh? People are nice. That's the nice thing about the world, my friend — people.

Incidentally, could anyone in his right mind ever guess that this simplistic drivel was written by the same man who, just two years later, produced one of the most brilliant scripts of all time, with some of the most heartbreakingly painful, razor-sharp and just plain unforgettable dialogue ever to grace the screen, speaking, of course, about Hart's rewrite of *A Star Is Born* (1954)? But then, Hart was on familiar ground there, having first tackled Hollywood expose 22 years before in *Once Upon a Lifetime;* here, as has already been pointed out, he was clearly out of his element.

Not only does Hart's script make Andersen out to be a fool and a weakling (this is not to say that Andersen wasn't a nice man in real life — though some accounts would challenge that assumption), but it has the audacity to derive much of its (rather weak) humor from precisely that premise. Typical examples are Peter's hastening a confused Hans to leave Odense for Copenhagen before the Burgomaster can arrive to tell him he's been banished from the town; Hans' sheepish refusal of the seamen's offer of hard liquor on boat to Copenhagen; and Hans' arriving with a new pair of shoes for the Ballerina just in time to miss their revelatory display of affection for each other and see the Ballet Director slap her (most of the other "laughs" are generated from this triangular situation).

Particularly disappointing is Hart's uncertain handling of an early scene in which the schoolmaster and council confront Hans about his "corrupting" the minds of the children with his stories. When the schoolmaster expresses indignation at Hans' anchoring the string of his kite to the history of Denmark, Hans replies, "The history of any country could always stand a little fresh air." And after the schoolmaster declares that "a cobbler belongs in his shop and children belong in a schoolroom," Hans rejoins with

> To be sure. But is the world made up of nothing but shoes and schoolrooms? There's a story, Burgomaster, of a piece of chalk and a blackboard. For years the piece of chalk had written so much on the blackboard that it began to think it knew everything. This made the blackboard unhappy because she felt that without her to write upon, no one would know anything, and she was the one who really knew it all. Well, one day, quite by accident, the schoolmaster broke the piece of chalk, and it landed right beside a pencil that the piece of chalk had always admired.

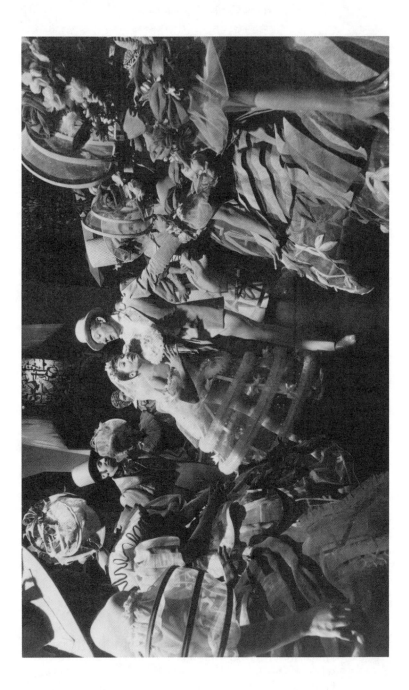

Because a pencil to a piece of chalk is something very special. Now, what do you suppose happened?

When the council members, who have been huddled around the Burgomaster, hanging on Hans' every word, ask in unison "What happened?" the schoolmaster promptly shatters their moment of rapture. This is supposed to register a big laugh, but it barely warrants a mild chuckle. The reason is that the alleged charm of Hans' little tale seems forced. Also, Hans never even reveals the ending—indeed, he admits he himself does not know what it is— and we do not understand how the story relates to the schoolmaster's argument. It turns out to be merely one of Hans' ruses for getting himself out of a tight spot. The problem here is that Hans' stories *do* seem genuinely silly and foolish, since it is difficult to understand how indeed the children learn from them, as he says they do. Therefore, we are forced to identify with the schoolmaster, of all people, which makes us even more uncomfortable since he is such a ridiculously drawn figure (one can easily imagine Goldwyn chuckling with glee, however, at his blustering manner—and at the cutesy finale in which he unabashedly asks Hans to sing "Thumbelina" for him).

As Crowther points out, it is only in song that we get a feel for the verbal genius for which Andersen was so well known. Frank Loesser's clever little patter songs are truly inspired— ingeniously intricate and wonderfully sprightly, completely worthy of the spirit of Andersen; indeed, if he had lived in the 20th century, he might have collaborated with Loesser on them—one thinks in particular of ditties like "Ugly Duckling," "Inchworm," "Thumbelina" and "The King's New Clothes." Not surprisingly, Loesser originally submitted to Goldwyn a score that was much longer—16 songs in all. But unfortunately, Goldwyn's insistence on including two ballet sequences precluded the use of all of them. The eight which remain are wonderful, of course, but more often than not they seem almost thrown away, as performed by Kaye in a too-subdued manner.

Opposite: *"No Two People": Danny Kaye and Jeanmaire.*

In particular, "Inchworm," "Thumbelina" and "Anywhere I Wander" are missing at least two choruses apiece, and the orchestrations on all except "No Two People" are at least partially inadequate, although Walter Scharf's arrangements of the background music are perfectly judged throughout. Those who wish to hear the songs in their entirety should purchase the MCA Records album entitled *Danny Kaye Sings Selections from the Samuel Goldwyn Technicolor Production "Hans Christian Andersen."* This is not a soundtrack album (that would have been a mistake, considering the orchestrations), but rather a specially recorded collection of the songs in their complete versions. Mercifully, Jane Wyman replaces the less-well-versed (in English, that is) Jeanmaire this time around.

But back to Hart's script. When he is not concentrating on his "pale, lumpish and wan" (Crowther) protagonist, he is supplying plenty of forced whimsy, sickeningly sentimental dialogue and heavy-handed exposition. Although there would not seem to be a precedent in Hart's resume for the inferior quality of his work here, in actuality the everpresent gooey sentimentality of the piece could be said to derive from his play *The Decision of Christopher Blake* (film version, 1948) — a sort of forerunner to *The Courtship of Eddie's Father* (1963) or *The Parent Trap* (1961) — in which a 12-year-old struggles to reunite his divorcing parents.

Hart's handling of the relationship between the Ballet Director and the Ballerina is particularly icky and embarrassing. He actually has the pair explain the reason for their frequent squabbles in no uncertain terms instead of allowing it to be implied through their actions. Niels: "Why is it that when you're dancing I see only my mortal enemy, the Ballerina?" Ballerina: "Because the ballet is your life just as it is mine. Don't you see, darling? It's just as it should be: professionally we fight like two tigers, but afterwards — that's what makes it so good, afterwards." (Again, this is the same man who wrote the exquisite proposal scene between Garland and Mason in *Star Is Born*!)

Such phrases as "Even half-starved I love you" and their constantly addressing each other as "darling" and "my love" make their scenes even harder to take — but most unbearable are the

Director's frequent adolescent jabs at his wife's alleged lack of dancing expertise, the most notable of which is undoubtedly "You dance the waltz like an elephant in a snowdrift."

Most appalling of all is the character of the Ballet Director (a role which is ironically perfectly suited to Farley Granger's propensity for gross overacting—prior to *Andersen,* he had marred two otherwise fine Hitchcock productions: *Rope,* 1948, and *Strangers on a Train,* 1951). Since Goldwyn had visions of the Powell-Pressburger classic of 1948, *The Red Shoes,* in his mind from the moment it was decided a sizable part of the picture would be devoted to elaborate ballets (more on that in a moment), it would not be unreasonable to assume that the Granger character was meant to resemble the autocratic impresario whom Anton Walbrook so elegantly articulated in the Powell film. If that is indeed the case, the comparison is about as fitting as likening the Bowery Boys to Sir Laurence Olivier.

Goldwyn's decision to give his picture a *Red Shoes* flavor did not stop with the Granger character. Moira Shearer, the star of the Powell film, had been his original choice for the part of the Ballerina, but she discovered at the last minute that she was pregnant, and so he was forced to replace her. The most obvious influence lies in having the story of the ballet (the Ballerina's discovery that she has sought love from the wrong man) paralleling that of the film (Hans believes that the Ballerina is miserable and will agree to run away with him as soon as she discovers that he "understands" her situation).

It is in this sense that Hart's having the Ballerina believe that Hans' disguised love letter is really a story for a ballet *is,* as Michael Freedland contests, a clever touch: the ballet itself then becomes a subjective experience when Hans is forced to envision it with only the music to guide him after being locked in a prop closet by Niels. In fact, Hans' final discovery that everything he had thought *was,* as Peter had said, pure fiction may even be an improvement (though purely on a *conceptual* level) over the finale of *Red Shoes,* which has always seemed forced and unmotivated (Victoria Page, the young dancer, is suddenly and inexplicably driven to her real death by her magical shoes, just as she was in the ballet).

Even Freedland, however, concedes that Goldwyn's motives in incorporating these elements into his picture were more pecuniary than aesthetic. In his determination to make *Hans* "the most important film he had shot since *Best Years* and one he hoped would possibly go down in history as the best to date" Goldwyn was determined to spare no expense. The picture was to cost in excess of $4,000,000 — $1.2 million more than *Oz*. Unfortunately, to Goldwyn size was the only way of assuring quality — not that the production suffered from overspending in the wrong areas, as would be the case with several later efforts in the genre, but rather that considering Goldwyn's incredibly naive ideas of what made a picture artistically successful, it's amazing that even a minute of good film was produced. The following anecdote from Freedland is particularly revealing:

> In planning the music for the "Little Mermaid" ballet, Goldwyn asked Walter Scharf, the picture's musical director, "How long was the longest ballet ever used in a picture?" Scharf thought he knew the answer but took his time to consult the books. It was the one Gene Kelly choreographed in *An American in Paris*. "How long was that?" asked Goldwyn. "Fourteen minutes," said the musician who wasn't used to assessing artistic success with a stop watch or a tape measure (actually, the ballet runs 17 minutes). "This one has got to be eighteen minutes," said the mogul. No mention of quality, of what sort of music would have to be written, how it was going to match the rest of the action and fit into the picture; just how long it was going to have to be.

Now, you can be sure that when Gene Kelly was planning that famous sequence from *American in Paris* the *last* thing on his mind was the number of minutes that he and Leslie Caron would be featured on screen. Kelly too derived his inspiration from the *Red Shoes* ballet and most likely sought to top or at least equal it, but the point is that while *he* worried about whether the style of the piece would correspond to that of Renoir or Toulouse-Lautrec, Goldwyn busied himself with buying a new stopwatch. In theory I should compare Goldwyn's motivations to those of Arthur Freed and Kelly's to those of choreographer Roland Petit, but Freed, to be sure, was just as much concerned with the aesthetic aspects of *American in Paris* as Kelly was, whereas Petit was pretty much left to his own designs after Goldwyn issued his mandate as to the ballet's length.

Luckily, Goldwyn had working under him several gifted artists who were possessed of enough intrinsic ability to transcend the meager and meaningless advice they received from their boss and produce quality work. Unfortunately, however, the director of the film, Charles Vidor, cannot be included among them. Vidor was most likely selected by Goldwyn because of his direction of one fairly successful musical biopic (of Chopin, *A Song to Remember* [1944]), and of one decent musical, *Cover Girl* (1944) — which in truth owed much more to the choreography of Gene Kelly and Stanley Donen, the dancing talents of Kelly and Rita Hayworth, and the comedy of Phil Silvers and Eve Arden than to any inspiration on the part of its director.

Goldwyn might also have been impressed by Vidor's ability for controlling Hayworth, a rather temperamental star whom Vidor had worked with especially well on 1946's *noir* classic *Gilda*, which is, as Rob Edelman puts it, "Vidor's one fascinating — and very atypical — credit." (*International Directory of Films and Filmmakers*, Vol. 2, p. 555). No doubt Goldwyn hoped Vidor would be able to hit it off with Danny Kaye, himself a rather difficult sort by reputation.

Vidor, despite what Goldwyn might have hoped, only seems to have assumed the position of a "yes-man" when it came to directing his star player — and the picture in general. Freedland quotes Walter Scharf as remembering the following:

> I think this was the only picture I've ever worked on where the choreographer was the actual star himself. Roland Petit only understood about ballet and was concentrating on the ballet movements. It was Danny himself who told Charles Vidor and [cinematographer] Harry Stradling where he was going to perform. I remember very vividly when we were doing the "Ugly Duckling" number how he schooled the little boy with the shaven head. He took him under his wing and put him at ease. He told Harry Stradling how he was going to use his hands. He was calling out all the shots. Danny planned the "Inchworm" number and arranged how the

children reciting their tables would work in counterpoint to the main melody. He designed the entry into Copenhagen — where there were 20 barkers, working against each other. I don't remember any film, including *Funny Girl* with Barbra Streisand, where the stars worked out everything.

It is interesting that Scharf and Stradling both were confronted with this sort of situation again, 16 years later, on *Funny Girl*. There, however, the director was strong-willed William Wyler, who continually fought with Streisand over her role as Fanny Brice, which she felt she knew better than anyone else after having played it over a thousand times on Broadway. That her performance was solid enough to win her the Best Actress Oscar that year is a good argument for Wyler's tenacity (Danny Kaye's performance in *Andersen* was not even acknowledged with a nomination, nor did it deserve one).

Vidor's influence on Kaye, if indeed he had any, was probably more negative than positive. Judging from the comments of Joey Walsh, who played Peter, Vidor was most likely at least partly responsible for the overly subdued manner which Kaye assumes for most of the picture. Walsh recalls that he himself felt somewhat "hampered by Vidor. I had natural enthusiasm, and I remember him saying to me in the early days of shooting — you know, I would say, 'Hey, Hans, we better get out of town. They're after us. We're in trouble, babe. You can't tell these stories to the kids' — 'Joey, I want no energy. I want you to tone it down.' So I said the line again, and he would say, 'No, take it down three times more than that, take it down some more,' and I would say the line and really drag it out.

"All I knew was that I felt reduced to almost nothing. So I slowly — as I saw that he was forgetting about me, with all the other things he had to do — started getting back my enthusiasm. He might, for all intensive purposes, have been trying to get something very fine out of me in terms of a performance, but it was just making me feel like 'I don't know what I'm doing now.' When I look at the picture now, I don't like myself in the first part, but as I went along I started to put more of myself into the role, like for instance things like pleading or getting angry, telling Hans that the Ballerina's making a fool out of him, that kind of thing. It might have been that Vidor looked at the dailies and saw that my performance with his direction wasn't working, and decided to let me go back to doing what I was doing at the beginning."

Walsh, who was then 14 (he is now 50 and a producer/screenwriter—of Altman's *California Split,* for example), does not remember his late co-star as being overbearing in the least, despite his domination of the director and crew: "Danny was terrific. He was almost a kid himself. He was a great prankster. I'll give you an example. He knew I couldn't stand sour cream beyond life itself, and there's a scene where we're sitting in the shop eating sour cream and rye bread, acting as if we like it. They were using real sour cream. All Danny had to do was find out that I hated the stuff. He blew that take eight times in a row! He goofed the last line in the scene up every time deliberately so that I'd have to eat this sour cream again. And my mother would complain, and he would say, 'I don't know what you're talking about, Mrs. Walsh. Have this woman removed from the set'. . .

"Also, Danny discovered early on when we were shooting the 'Wonderful Copenhagen' number that I couldn't sing *at all.* If you look at the scene closely, you will see great embarrassment in my face. So Danny said, 'Joey, try to *mouth* these things. You are the worst singer I've ever heard.' So I ended up whispering it. Danny pulled no punches with me just because I was 14, but it was all done lovingly. In fact, after the picture was finished, he sent me a very nice telegram that said, 'Joey, maybe 10, 15 years later you'll play the cobbler and I'll play the kid. We'll do a remake!'"

Getting back to Vidor's direction of the film in general, with regard to the musical numbers—if they can indeed be called that, nondescript as most of them are—again Crowther is right on the money (he even guesses correctly that the star had a lot to do with their creation): "All these items seem strung together, like trinkets on a chain. Mr. Kaye and Charles Vidor have plunked them with no dramatic flow." With the exception of "No Two People," the "Dream Fantasy" and the two ballets, the "Ice Skating" one and "The Little Mermaid," there really isn't a hell of a lot to comment upon.

According to Joey Walsh, the "Inchworm" number, in which Kaye serenades an unseen inchworm as the children inside the adjacent schoolhouse laboriously recite their arithmetic tables and which takes up no more than a minute and a half of screen time, incredibly took some *nine hours* to get right! Now, Kaye's concept for the bit *is* somewhat clever, but there is absolutely no tension in the rather dreary little segment, since the set-up is so simplistic (there is not even a need for crosscutting between the children and Kaye, since they are clearly heard in voice-over), and the song seems thrown away.

"The King's New Clothes" resolves itself into another of Hans' before-school stories for the children, who gather around him on a grassy bank near a river.

"I'm Hans Christian Andersen," the title song, is broken up and used at various points throughout the film, the most memorable of which has Kaye appearing at the doorway of the shop after learning that one of his stories is to be published, waltzing across the room ballet-style, picking up a chair and serenading it in time to the lyrics.

"Wonderful Copenhagen" is Hans' and Peter's salute to the magical city they see before them as they look off into the distance from the ship's bow.

"Thumbelina" has Hans entertaining a lonely little girl outside his cell window by creating the title character from a handkerchief wrapped around his painted thumb.

Hans sings the story of "The Ugly Duckling" to cheer up a small boy who has had his head shaved because of an operation.

"Anywhere I Wander" finds Hans dreaming of the Ballerina as he sits outside his shop one evening.

All of the aforementioned are done in simple camera setups with little or no imagination in the staging (proof that the star needed either a strong director or choreographer, or both), and most fail to register much of an impact on the viewer, although "The King's New Clothes," "Thumbelina" and particularly "The Ugly Duckling" are charming, and "Wonderful Copenhagen" is given a measure of zest by Kaye's vigorous rendition.

The real highlights of the picture are the "Dream Fantasy" with Kaye, Granger and Jeanmaire, "No Two People" with Kaye and Jeanmaire, Jeanmaire's ice-skating ballet and, of course, the final "Little Mermaid" ballet featuring her and husband Roland Petit. Each of these evidences an inventiveness and a confidence in the staging which contrasts sharply with Vidor's rather limp handling of the rest of the picture and indicates that Roland Petit must have been involved at least to some degree on the staging of "Dream Fantasy" and "No Two People."

"Dream Fantasy" (which for many years was left out of the 104-minute prints of the film which have been circulating but was recently restored) is a deliciously choreographed bit which finds Hans wandering through a bizarre maze reminiscent of something from the *Red Shoes* ballet in search of the Ballerina. After bursting through a closed doorway, he finds her husband torturously rehearsing her. In an effort to rescue her, Hans grabs a sword and duels with Niels, killing him, after which the Ballerina rushes into his waiting arms.

The tone here is plainly tongue-in-cheek, and is the only real opportunity in the film for Kaye to display some of the wild physical antics which had made him famous in such earlier pics as *Up in Arms* (1944), *The Kid from Brooklyn* (1946) and, most memorably, *The Secret Life of Walter Mitty* (1947). The deliberately exaggerated comedy of the number ironically points up the unintentional ludicrousness of the characterizations in general as essayed by Hart—particularly, as mentioned before, that of the Ballet Director.

"No Two People" is pretty much in the same vein, with Hans and the Ballerina wedding each other in a cake-frosting setting and gently mocking their apparent bliss as they work their way through the song.

"The Little Mermaid" ballet is, as most people agree, the artistic summit of the film—and indeed it should be, considering that Goldwyn lavished more than $400,000 of the film's budget on it. It is here that, as Crowther notes, "the latent excitement in the picture is brought to a momentary boil [as] Jeanmaire, amid a bright company of spinning beauties and some dreamy ballet decor, [mercifully] nips the focus of audience attention and excitement right away from Danny Kaye."

Crowther perceptively describes Petit's style as "modern

Top: *"Dream Ballet": Jeanmaire, Farley Granger, Danny Kaye.* Bottom: *Couples dance in the prince's palace in the "Little Mermaid" ballet sequence.*

graphic." At no time, however, does it approach the daring, flamboyance or extravagance of Powell, Kelly or Vincente Minnelli (one would be hard pressed to find a single film history text which even makes note of Petit's work here in its chapter on screen dancing), although one effect — Jeanmaire's clutching the magic veil that will make her human, twirling about and suddenly appearing in a white wedding gown — seems intended to rival Moira Shearer's sudden leap into the red shoes, which magically lace themselves around her feet, in Powell's film.

Although there are intense moments — particularly the dance in the Prince's ballroom with couples leaping over tables and Jeanmaire's threatening the unfaithful Prince with a knife which she instead uses on herself — there is nothing to equal the sinister aura of Leonide Massine's Shoemaker, or Shearer glissading through a sea of falling cellophane (a deficiency which would have seemed all the more pronounced had Shearer been able to star in *Hans* as originally planned). Jeanmaire, however, does very well by the role of the mermaid, as does Mr. Petit with his Prince (there is probably more actual screen time devoted to dancing here than in *The Red Shoes*'s ballet, which relied on numerous special effects and clever camerawork to an unusual degree).

Walter Scharf's score, a highly complicated arrangement of several pieces of music by Liszt which he nevertheless managed to make seem an original piece of work, lends the appropriate romantic/tragic atmosphere to the piece, but I myself prefer the less conventional, dark-edged strains of Brian Easdale's score for *The Red Shoes*. The important point to remember here is that Michael Powell and company (including choreographer Robert Helpmann) were consciously setting out to make an art film, whereas Goldwyn, as mentioned earlier, conceived of merely an escapist entertainment with artistic pretensions — nor did Goldwyn have under his wing the ingenious collaborators whom the Archers regularly employed on their productions.

It is Scharf's arrangement of Loesser's background score which occasionally makes up for the lax direction of Vidor, as when Peter finally manages to entice Hans to journey to Copenhagen: "Think of what a to-do there'll be! They'll talk of nothing

else for days — 'Hans has gone to Copenhagen.'" The musical accompaniment creates a momentary surge of excitement and anticipation in the viewer as Hans stands at the doorway, con-
templating leaving. To Vidor's credit, however, he does manage
a nice touch here and there, such as the opening crane shot
which follows Hans' kite downward to the bank where the children are gathered, then tilts up to the right to reveal the kite's
owner. And despite everything, the picture does not drag half as
much as one would expect.

The other technical credits on the picture are not terribly
impressive: Richard Day's sets do, as Pauline Kael writes, have
the air of "blowsy, cheap-calendar decor" (the first view of
Copenhagen as seen from the deck of Hans and Peter's ship recalls the matte shot of Emerald City in *Oz*), and Harry Stradling's
cinematography lends a certain glossiness to the production but
little else.

In view of the final product, Goldwyn's original intention to
make *Hans* his best film to date seems laughable, to say the least.
However, in spite of the far-less-than-favorable impression of the
picture which has no doubt conveyed thus far, I still harbor a certain fondness for it. Although, as David Shipman notes, the mixture of sentiment and whimsy is at times "nauseating" (for which
one must blame Moss Hart's syrupy script above all else), and, as
Leslie Halliwell points out, overall the picture is an "artificial,
sugary confection with little humor and far too little magic of any
kind," and despite the fact that it really has little to do with Hans
Christian Andersen and Danny Kaye is basically miscast in the
title role, the film is still an amiable affair, and has enough attractive and charming elements (mainly Frank Loesser's tunes and
the ballet excerpts) to appeal to the imaginations of adults
(though decidedly not the most discerning ones) and children
alike. However, it does not even come close to *The Wizard of Oz*
in terms of artistic success or adherence to the requirements of
a good children's live-action musical film. As we shall see, the
next feature to be discussed, *The 5000 Fingers of Dr. T*, marks a
step up from *Hans* on both these levels.

The 5000 Fingers of Dr. T

A Stanley Kramer Company Production, released by Columbia Pictures, 1953. *Producer* Stanley Kramer. *Director* Roy Rowland. *Screenplay* Dr. Seuss, Allan Scott. *Story and Conception by* Dr. Seuss. *Director of Photography* Franz Planer, A.S.C. *Technicolor Color Consultant* Francis Cugat. *Production Designer* Rudolph Sternad. *Music* Frederick Hollander. *Musical Director* Morris Stoloff. *Lyrics* Dr. Seuss. *Choreography* Eugene Loring. *Miss Healy's Gowns* Jean Louis. *Art Director* Cary Odell. *Editorial Supervision* Harry Gerstad. *Production Manager* Clem Beauchamp. *Film Editor* Al Clark, A.C.E. *Set Decorations* William Kiernan. *Assistant Director* Frederick Briskin. *Hairstyles* Helen Hunt. *Makeup* Clay Campbell. *Sound Engineer* Russell Malmgren. Technicolor. Running Time: 88 minutes.

Cast Peter Lind Hayes (Zabladowski), Mary Healy (Mrs. Collins), Hans Conreid (Dr. Terwilliker), Tommy Rettig (Bart), John Heasley (Uncle Whitney), Robert Heasley (Uncle Judson), Noel Cravat (Sergeant Lunk), Henry Kulky (Stroogo).

Songs and Musical Numbers "Ten Happy Fingers," "Dream Stuff," "Hypnotic Duel," "Get Together Weather," "The Kids' Song," "Dungeon Ballet," "Victorious," "Dungeon Elevator," "The Dressing Song."

In his *Film and Video Guide,* critic Leslie Halliwell observes that *The 5000 Fingers of Dr. T* was a "real oddity to have come from Hollywood at this time" (the time being 1953). What is even stranger is that the film was produced by Stanley Kramer, who had been largely if not single-handedly responsible for the then-prevalent cycle of socially conscious productions, among them *Champion* (1949), *Home of the Brave* (1949) and *The Men* (1950). The truth is that Kramer had committed himself to the project back in 1947, before his first independent production, *So This Is New York* (1948), had ever been released.

Opening dream sequence: Tommy Rettig and goons.

Kramer had been approached by Theodor (Ted) Geisel, better known as "Dr. Seuss," a well-known author of bizarre and unimaginable children's books like *The 5000 Hats of Bartholomew Cubbins, And To Think That I Saw It on Mulberry Street, Horton Hears a Who, Horton Hatches the Egg* and *Thidwick, the Big-Hearted Moose.* By 1952, Geisel was himself no stranger to the motion picture business, having just won an Academy Award for his cartoon "Gerald McBoing-Boing." He had come up with a concept for a major feature film based upon two leftover ideas in his notebook. First, he harbored a lingering hatred for forcible systems of teaching little boys to play the piano, and second, he simply found the notion of two men with a Siamese beard intensely diverting.

Kramer had vowed that if he ever had a couple million dollars, he would be happy to make a film based upon those seemingly incongruous notions. Finally, in 1951, Kramer found himself in possession of $25,000,000 of Columbia Pictures' money, to use pretty much as he pleased, and he promptly summoned the reclusive author down from his loft in LaJolla, California. Kramer was eager to do something different from the rather drab, depressing fare he had offered audiences thus far (this would be his first color film). He told Donald Spoto that "It was one of my favorite properties, and one which I very much wanted to direct myself. Columbia Pictures wasn't ready for that yet, and there wasn't enough money to do what should really have been a musical extravaganza."

Nevertheless, the $2,000,000 budget on the picture was hardly a meager one by 1952 standards, and the major creative talents whom Kramer managed to secure for what was essentially a kid's film (though hopefully with enough sophisticated elements to keep the adults interested as well) were nothing to sneeze at either: cinematographer Franz (here billed as "Frank") Planer, who had helped to recreate the Vienna of old for Max Ophuls in what turned out to be Ophuls' best film, *Letter from an Unknown Woman* (1948); composer Frederick Hollander, who had written the famous "Falling in Love Again" for Marlene Dietrich in *The Blue Angel* (1930) and also the score for Billy Wilder's similar *Foreign Affair* (1948), also starring Dietrich; choreographer Eugene Loring and production designer Rudolph Sternad.

The film's opening moments find nine-year-old Bart Collins (Tommy Rettig) wandering lost through a dream world of huge metallic balls and mounds set on a slick, gunmetal floor. As he moves over the oddly constructed universe, he is attacked from all sides by a group of darkly clad men wielding colorful nets just the right size for ensnaring small boys. As the pursuers close in on him, the picture fades out and in again to reveal the boy, asleep at a piano. As he screams for the nightmare to vanish, he is awakened by his piano teacher, Dr. Terwilliker (Hans Conreid), a mean, pedantic dictator whose only concern seems to be preparing his students for an upcoming recital, and who will not let "one dreary little boy" humiliate him. He further demands that Bart practice, practice, practice until his technique is perfect.

After Dr. Terwilliker stomps out the door, Bart turns and addresses the camera directly: "Well, that's my problem," he says. "Dr. T is the only enemy I've got." He further explains that he accepts this horrid situation only because it pleases his mother, who is having a difficult time of it since the death of his father.

Mrs. Collins (Mary Healy) enters and proceeds to reprimand her son for not practicing. The plumber, Zabladowski (Peter Lind Hayes), enters also, bearing a new kitchen sink. He brashly starts to side with Bart in the argument, but also receives a reprimand from the mother. She tells Zabladowski to mind his own business and informs him that Bart will learn to play the piano "if I have to keep him at that keyboard forever."

"Dr. Terwilliker has my mom hypnotized," Bart informs the audience as his head sways groggily with the movements of the metronome. Suddenly he drifts off again . . . and finds himself seated at an enormously high piano. On a podium far above his head stands Dr. T beating with a baton at an ever-increasing pace. With a sinister chuckle, Terwilliker informs Bart that tomorrow his dream will be fulfilled—that tomorrow 500 little boys will be seated at the giant piano in Terwilliker's "Happy Fingers Institute" practicing 24 hours a day, 365 days a year—and that the 5000 little fingers will be "mine, all mine."

Terwilliker points for Bart to go to his cell and leaves. The bewildered Bart crosses the courtyard and enters a dark alley. He spies his dog, but the dog runs away. Voices call out of the darkness, telling him the evils of Terwilliker's prison. And out of all this, Bart spies Zabladowski as he comes down the alley carrying a sink.

Zabladowski explains that he has the job of installing 500 sinks for the 500 little boys, but says he guesses Bart will be all right "so long as your ma's here." Because, he continues, Mrs. Collins is in the No. 2 spot—as Terwilliker's right-hand "man."

The plumber disappears and Bart continues down the alley into a big room where he is almost trapped by a rope strung across the entrance. He looks to either side and sees that the "rope" is a long white beard, connected at either end by a forbidding-looking twin (Jack and Bob Heasley). The twins scare

Dr. T demonstrates to Bart and Zabladowski what happens to those who fail to obey his orders.

Bart out of his boots as they menace him with a fantastic skating routine, finally driving him from the room.

Bart flounders through corridor after corridor, through manholes and up seemingly topless stairways until he reaches his mother, who assures him that he'll learn to love all this. He also learns that his mother is under Terwilliker's hypnotic spell and that the "piano-monster plans to marry her."

Meanwhile, Terwilliker learns that Bart is not in his cell and sends the terrible Sergeant Lunk (Noel Cravat) and his soldiers to find the boy. Sirens wail, searchlights gleam as the hunt goes on. Time and again he slides down bannisters, through manholes and races down dark corridors. Bart is nearly captured. But he finally winds up in a dungeon, surrounded by moldy musicians of every variety. Terwilliker has imprisoned all musicians who do not play the piano.

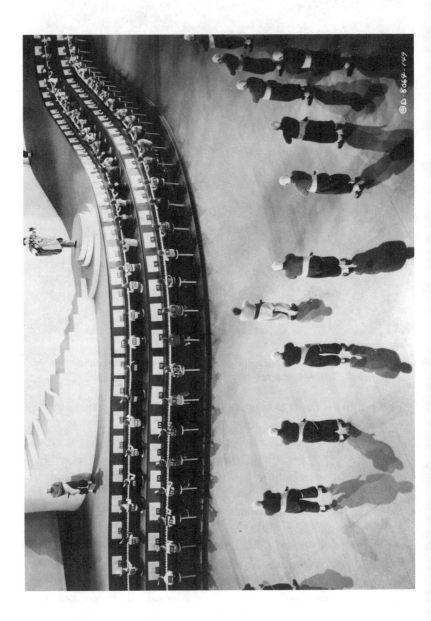

Escaping from the dungeon, Bart finds Zabladowski and enlists his aid to help break the hypnotic spell Terwilliker holds over Mrs. Collins. The plumber and Mrs. Collins meet and fall in love immediately. However, Terwilliker breaks it up by again hypnotizing Mrs. Collins. He is unable to conquer Zabladowski, but he appeals to the man's friendship and finally wins over the plumber.

Bart overhears Terwilliker giving orders that the plumber be disintegrated at dawn and runs to tell Zabladowski. The plumber, however, refuses to believe him. But with persuasion Bart wins over the man and, with a promise of more money than Terwilliker is paying, Zabladowski agrees to take out the sinks he already has installed. If the sinks aren't there Terwilliker will be thwarted. The city sanitary code will not permit him to house the 500 little boys.

Seeing the soldiers coming, Bart races around corners, under sliding doors, up split staircases and finally comes to Terwilliker's bedroom. There he finds a certificate of assassination, ordering Zabladowski's death at dawn. He runs away with the soldiers in hot pursuit.

Bart rushes through the cell block and hears the voice of his mother. Terwilliker, who fears that she will escape from the hypnotic trance, has locked her up. His dog appears, but betrays him by barking. He scales walls, climbs over ledges and finally grabs a hanging rope which is disclosed to be the beard of the twins. In horror he leaps again—right into the arms of the soldiers.

There is only one avenue of escape. He runs up a topless sky ladder. The searchlights pick him out as he appears far above the buildings. He can't go down. So Bart pulls the bottom of his seat out of his trousers and makes a perfect parachute jump, landing in the alley.

Bart finds Zabladowski and shows him the certificate of assassination. The plumber now knows the boy is on the level, but Bart demands that they seal their bond of friendship in blood. Jabbing their thumbs with a pin, Bart administers the oath and

Opposite: *The enormous piano at which 500 boys sit, under the command of Dr. T.*

Zabladowski wraps band-aids around their respective thumbs. In the eyes of Bart, the plumber is now his "pop."

Together they steal through the darkness to a new land—a land filled with Mound Country men armed with searchlights and butterfly nets. After nearly being captured they escape and rescue Mrs. Collins. In the chase that follows they encounter the terrible twins with the Siamese beard. After a terrific struggle, Zabladowski takes out a pair of shears and snips the beard. The twins collapse to the floor. Just as Bart is about the feel the thrill of victory, Terwilliker appears. He puts Mrs. Collins back into the hypnotic trance and hurries Bart and Zabladowski away to a dungeon. Here they are all alone, except for a terrible-looking guard wearing a hearing aid.

Bart complains of the smell and Zabladowski immediately produces from his pocket a bottle of chlorophyll Air-Fix. Bart gets an idea. If this bottle will pull smell out of the air, why not invent a Music-Fix that will pull music out of the air? Together the inventors go to work, tossing everything in their pockets into the bottle and winding up with the hearing aid from the ear of the sleeping guard. Then they pull the cork and talk. There is no sound—it works. With this little device, Bart can put the big piano on the fritz.

Next morning 500 unhappy little boys are seated at the piano. Above them stands Terwilliker on the podium, about to conduct his greatest work. On the downbeat Bart pulls the cork of the Music-Fix. Five thousand fingers strike the keyboard, but there is no sound. Again and again the maestro tries—but no sound. The Bart inserts the cork and the resounding melody rolls forth.

Waving the bottle, Bart assures Terwilliker that it is atomic. Four little boys grab their menace and hurl him into a dungeon. Then Bart conducts the assembled group in "the most beautiful piece ever written"—Chopsticks.

But too much music has been crammed into the bottle. It begins to smoke. Five hundred boys scatter as the atomic blast fills the room. Bart is suddenly blown back to reality. Zabladowski is shaking the dozing boy before the piano. Mrs. Collins appears in the room. For the first time in real life she and the

plumber notice one another. Somehow, Bart and Zabladowski
are still wearing their bandages. Bart grabs his baseball glove to
go outside, turning the pictures of Terwilliker on the music face
down.

With this film we return to the basic structure of *Wizard of
Oz:* a fantastic centerpiece framed by a reality which initially
seems oppressive but which turns out to be vastly preferable to
the imagined world. Once again our protagonist is a small
child — though, of course, this time it is a young boy. In this case,
however, we are treated to a much shorter prologue (five
minutes as opposed to *Oz*'s 20) before entering the dream world,
and the means by which we are encouraged to identify with Bart
Collins' predicament differ also from the techniques employed in
Oz.

This time, instead of the normal third-person narrative
structure, we have the young hero addressing the camera directly,
an act which draws us into his own level of experience with a
minimum of effort (this only occurs at the outset, however; Bart
does not narrate the film). Like Dorothy, Bart is an orphan, and
feels trapped and isolated in an environment where no one
understands him. His dream is an extreme projection of this
situation (the corridors of Terwilliker's "Happy Fingers Institute"
seem endless, as does the master piano which seats the 500 boys
at the film's climax).

As in *Oz*, the central character's fears are crystallized in the
form of one hideous individual — here it is Dr. Terwilliker. However, in this case the villain's motives for pursuing the protagonist
are basically the same in both the real and fantasy worlds (they
both involve Bart's playing the piano at a recital), whereas in *Oz*
the subplot with the ruby slippers had to be created once
Dorothy landed in Oz: the screenwriters obviously felt that the
Witch's desiring a small dog would seem slightly ridiculous —
though they did have her remark at one point, "Drat you and your
dog. You've been more trouble to me than you're worth, one way
or another. But it'll soon be over now." The connection between
the Witch and Terwilliker is made most explicit when, after Bart
and company succeed in conquering the Siamese twins and are

on the verge of escaping, Terwilliker appears at the top of a stair-case, just in time to stop them — an almost perfect duplication of a scene in *Oz*.

The most striking and significant difference between the two films resides in the nature and treatment of the fantasy se-quences. The word "sophisticated" is often used in connection with *5000 Fingers of Dr. T* (usually to describe the dream se-quences), and for that reason deserves some mention here. Like *Oz*, there was an attempt with *5000 Fingers of Dr. T* to make a picture that would be enticing enough to lure the kiddie au-dience in, while ostensibly providing at the same time enough thought-provoking elements to keep the adults happy (and awake). Unfortunately, as Daniel Einstein points out in his article on the film in *Magill's Survey of Cinema*, the picture proved to be more of a hit with kids than with their parents, since the latter "have [already] worked through, exorcised or repressed the many childhood fears brought to light in the film, [whereas] children have not yet had the chance to do so. [Therefore] to a small child whose eyes are not yet jaded and whose brain has not as yet become sophisticated enough to see through the . . . Freud-ianisms . . . viewing the picture can be an extremely frightening experience." Incidentally, this could have been one of the reasons that the picture flopped at the box office: the major target audience in 1953 was not children and teens (as it is now) but rather adults over the age of 30.

The reader will recall that in *Oz*, Dorothy's situation was always kept from becoming too frightening or disturbing (the limit being as mentioned in Chapter 1, the moment when the Witch's image replaces Aunt Em's in the crystal ball), mainly paralleling the conventional fears of most children, foremost be-ing that of finding oneself unable to get home once one has lost his way. Here, however, we are dealing with the mind of Dr. Seuss, that master purveyor of the bizarre. Somewhat regret-tably, this time out Seuss trades in his penchant for tongue-twisters (with the exception of the lyrics for the film's songs) to indulge his taste for queer situations and characters.

Seuss has a field day peppering his script with elementary Freudian overtones (the most disturbing involving the poor soul who, as punishment for disobeying Dr. T, is forced to remain trapped inside a huge white drum, beating away with a mallet), which capitalize on basic childhood fears. The result, as Pauline Kael comments, seems to have backfired somewhat, in the sense that the younger audience came to enjoy — to an unhealthy degree — such horrific elements: "unfortunately, good, progressive parents, knowing that this was a Stanley Kramer production, from a script by Dr. Seuss, took their children to see it, and thus heard their kids scream with fear and excitement (the kids didn't take their parents with them when they went to see *Psycho*)."

To my mind, at any rate, Seuss' astounding popularity has always seemed somewhat baffling, since his brand of humor would seem to be an esoteric one, an acquired taste. It is hard to put one's finger on exactly what he hoped to achieve with this picture (or with many of his other writings, for that matter). If it was simply to entertain children, then what type of child was he aiming at? Donald Spoto, who wrote a critique of the film in his *Stanley Kramer: Film Maker,* wondered about this also when he expressed uncertainty at composer Frederick Hollander's labeling the film "an unusual child's opera for adults." Spoto: "I can't help wondering what's 'unusual' — the child or the opera?"

His books are popular first and foremost because of their challenging (to those learning to read) language, not necessarily for their content. Those adults who at an advanced age find they can still quote passages from them verbatim usually take pride in that accomplishment alone, and very rarely stop to consider the considerably unsettling images those words conjure up. I am thinking particularly of titles like *Bartholomew and the Oobleck,* in which an entire village is engulfed by a thick goo. Typically, most people seem to remember only relatively harmless tales like *Cat in the Hat* or *Green Eggs and Ham* — no doubt because, as Einstein says, they have exorcized the fears those other stories may have aroused at any early age.

To say that Seuss has an odd sense of humor is a gross understatement. Who else would delight in having one of his characters (the plumber, Zabladowski) take a swig of *pickle juice* in order to give himself the requisite energy to battle his antagonists (in this case, the bearded twins)? Or have Bart and the plumber take a blood oath to cement their friendship—and then have Bart use this as an excuse to call Zabladowski "Pop" and have him thereby refer to Mrs. Collins as his "wife"? Granted, this is a projection of an unconscious desire for family stability on Bart's part, but the way it is manifested seems strange, to say the least.

Much of the humor is self-conscious, as though the characters (Zabladowski in particular) are aware that they are appearing in Bart's dream. While this technique evoked a warm smile of recognition in the viewer in *Oz*, as employed here it is hard to work up any sort of emotional response to it—or to any of the characters in the film either. Part of the reason for this has to do with Seuss' inability (shared by his co-scriptwriter Allan Scott) to construct a scenario which could sustain an audience's interest for 90 minutes (after which one begins to grow decidedly uneasy about Seuss' sinister ruminations—a feeling which is not eased by the close resemblance between Frederick Hollander's eerie score and Miklos Rozsa's music for *The Lost Weekend* (1945).

In short, the script lacks an overall sense of urgency and direction, appearing to have been constructed instead in fits and spurts (with Seuss trying to jam every bizarre idea he had not yet used in somewhere). This could be attributed to the fact that the picture was originally considerably longer (it contained 24 songs), having been cut by the distributor, Columbia, to a length deemed more suitable for a kid's picture. However, the same criticism most likely held true for the first cut.

Although we learn at the outset that the grand opening of Terwilliker's "Happy Fingers Institute" is only a day away, most of the remainder until the climax with the recital is taken up with Bart and or Zabladowski and Mrs. Collins being chased about the prisonlike Institute by assorted goons, an idea which quickly grows tiresome. Much of the time there is a lack of a real center of interest, making the picture seem empty. In addition, the song numbers are never more than an instrusion, as they stop the film dead in its tracks, and do not advance the plot (there is also some pointless dialogue with Bart and Zabladowski arguing over his salary—although with an occasional redeeming line, like

Zabladowski's remark after defeating Terwilliker in an intense swordfight; "Oh, that. I just picked it up."). Of course, the fact that Mrs. Collins, Bart and Zabladowski are separated from each other for much of the duration does not help matters much, either (Mary Healy doesn't appear on screen for much more than 10 minutes total).

Other faults with the script: the point of the opening sequence is questionable, as it seems to have been inserted merely to show that Bart is a dreamer—a fact which we discover soon enough anyway. Also, the very same creatures featured in this opening segment reappear later in the film, so the initial sequence seems merely superfluous. There is also uncertainty about the ending—why should we believe that Bart is, as Einstein argues, "freed at last from the horrors of the piano and of Dr. Terwilliker"?

While Seuss hints (by revealing that Bart and Zabladowski are still wearing their bandages) that this may not have been a dream, he does not give Mrs. Collins anything to say which would indicate that she has given up her ambition that her son become a great pianist like his two uncles (a reference which is missing in the extant cut version—one does not therefore recognize that the Siamese twins in the dream are the counterparts of the uncles), nor is there any reason to assume that Dr. T will not return tomorrow for another lesson. Strangely enough, this problem with the ending recalls a very similar situation with *Oz:* though many people overlook this, the Miss Gulch–Toto crisis of the first two reels, as Doug McClelland has pointed out, is left unresolved at the climax. Are we supposed to assume that Dr. T and Miss Gulch have been wiped out in real life just as they were in the dream sequences? There is definitely a loose plot thread dangling in both cases.

If Seuss' treatment of the subject seems questionable, he is not aided by the film's director, Roy Rowland, whose "style" lacks even the occasional flair of Charles Vidor; Rowland's filmography (which includes things like *Meet Me in Las Vegas*) is without exception undistinguished. It is hard to imagine why Kramer chose him for the project (presumably because he had directed children fairly well in some of his earlier pics, the titles of which really aren't worth mentioning), but at least he has admitted his mistake: "Roy Rowland was perhaps not the right director. The picture required a tougher man. The idea of the film is not a gentle one. It's an attack on a life-style, but you wouldn't know it from what you see." It is from witnessing such directorial indifference that one comes to appreciate all the more the total emotional commitment of someone as seemingly impersonal as Victor Fleming.

Most disappointing perhaps are the performances, if indeed they can be labeled as such. Little Tommy Rettig is on screen most of the time, and although he is agreeable, he is nothing more, and his insistent goody-goody optimism tends to grate on one's nerves after a while (the fact that the film's final image — Rettig running out the front door with his baseball bat and dog in tow — recalls his association with the television show *Lassie* does not help his case either). Peter Lind Hayes, as Zabladowski, has absolutely no screen presence (this was, thankfully, the Vegas entertainer's only film role), and his wife, Mary Healy, as mentioned before, is onscreen for so little time that it is hard to say anything of significance about her (though she shows some early promise when she sings "Ten Happy Fingers" to Rettig). The one bright spot is the late Hans Conreid as Dr. T, with his "throatily gleeful male witch's voice" (Spoto). Conreid has a few choice lines, such as his tongue-in-cheek lament at the demise of the Siamese twins: "Alas, poor Judson and Whitney. I knew them well." The thinness of the other characterizations, however, makes it hard for one to stick with and therefore care about the principals as they go about their business.

There are exactly two sequences in the film which are worth noting for their inventiveness and or tight handling, and they are, not surprisingly, the segments which receive honorable mention in almost all critiques of this film, which has become something of a cult item. First and foremost is the "Dungeon Ballet," the credit for which should go entirely to choreographer Eugene Loring. For more than five minutes, the main action of the picture stops and we the audience are treated to a *truly* sophisticated and imaginative sequence in which a group of miserable creatures, grown green and moldy with age and imprisoned because they dared play instruments other than the piano, blissfully accompany themselves on instruments fashioned from all kinds of odd materials (a mannequin is used as a violin, for example). It is here that Hollander's contribution to the film is most appreciated also, so soothing are his melodies. Like all good filmed ballets, however, the piece is really impossible to describe in words, and really must be seen (and heard).

The other important sequence is a bit more predictable: the final recital. Peter Lind Hayes recalls that Roy Rowland became ill during the shooting of this longish scene, and that Kramer himself took over (though the numerous second-unit directors no doubt contributed to the final effect also). The rapid cutting here as Bart thwarts Dr. T's attempts to conduct by opening and closing his Music-Fix holds one's attention, but at no time could be labeled Hitchcockian (many of the shots don't seem to be judged properly in terms of point of view).

Other factors worth mentioning: Rudolph Sternad's sets and Franz Planer's cinematography have been said by Spoto and others to evoke German expressionism, particularly Robert Wiene's 1919 *The Cabinet of Dr. Caligari.* The comparisons would seem more fitting to me had *Dr. T* been photographed in black and white also. However, to Planer's credit, he did manage to lend the film a queasy, neurotic feel which distinguishes it from the merely glossy look of *Oz* and *Hans*—and Sternad's sets often manage to merge cartoonlike fantasy and realism into one seamless whole (in particular the ladder which Bart climbs to the sky).

All in all *The 5000 Fingers of Dr. T* would seem to exist on an artistic plane a step above *Hans Christian Andersen* and at least two below *Oz.* Technically it is far more imaginative than *Hans*, and is never cloying or overly sentimental—its tone, on the contrary, as I have said, is oftentimes either too sinister or just plain *weird* for most tastes (which explains why it is only infrequently revived in theaters and on television). The motifs present in this story—overthrowing an evil force, for example—which are a throwback to *Oz*, will reappear in later efforts like *tom thumb, Babes in Toyland, Chitty Chitty Bang Bang, Pufnstuf* and *Bedknobs and Broomsticks.*

tom thumb

A Galaxy/George Pal Production, *released by* Metro-Goldwyn-Mayer, 1958. *Producer and Director* George Pal. *Associate Producer* Dora Wright. *Screenplay* Ladislas Fodor, *based on a story from the pen of* the Brothers Grimm. *Director of Photography* Georges Perinal, A.S.C. *Photographic effects* Tom Howard, F.R.P.S. *Film Editor* Frank Clarke. *Costume Designer* Olga Lehmann. *Art Director* Elliott Scott. *Production Manger* E.J. Holding. *Assistant Director* David Middlemas. *Camera Operator* Denys Coop. *Animators* Gene Warren, Wah Chang, Don Sahlin, Herb Johnson. *Music Direction* Muir Mathieson. *Musical Score* Douglas Gamley, Ken Jones. *Recording Supervisor* A.W. Watkins. *Sound Recording* John Bramall. *Continuity* Angela Martelli. *Makeup* Charles Parker. *Hairdresser* Hilda Fox. Technicolor. Running Time: 92 minutes.

Cast Russ Tamblyn (tom thumb), Alan Young (Woody), June Thorburn (Forest Queen), Terry-Thomas (Ivan), Peter Sellers (Tony), Bernard Miles (tom's Father), Jessie Matthews (tom's Mother), Ian Wallace (Shoemaker), Peter Butterworth (Bandmaster), Peter Bull (Town Crier), Barbara Ferris (Thumbella), Stan Freberg (Yawning Man's voice), Dal McKennon (Con-Fu-Shon's voice), the Puppetoons.

Songs "tom thumb's tune," "Are You a Dream" by Peggy Lee; "The Talented Shoes" and "After All These Years" by Fred Spielman and Janice Torre; "The Yawning Song" by Fred Spielman and Kermit Goell.

tom thumb was the brainchild of special effects wizard George Pal (1908–1980), who had previously won Academy awards for his work in the motion pictures *Destination Moon* (1950), *When Worlds Collide* (1951) and the ever-popular sci-fi classic *War of the Worlds* (1953). *tom* was to be Pal's first film as director (he had only supervised the other productions), as well as an opportunity for him to show off his "Puppetoons"—puppet-cartoons utilizing stop-action animation—in an extensive

Russ Tamblyn as tom with some of George Pal's Puppetoons.

format (the creations were first introduced by Pal in the 1940s and featured in a series for Paramount; he received his first Oscar for them in 1944). Pal had been trying to get MGM to back *tom thumb* for years; finally, in 1957, the studio relented on two conditions. One was that Russ Tamblyn, a young actor-dancer from Broadway and MGM contractee, play the role of tom and not Donald O'Connor, who badly wanted it and who Pal had agreed would be perfect in it. The second was that the film, because of its estimated $2 million budget, would have to be made at MGM's British studio (where Gene Kelly had recently completed work on his *Invitation to the Dance,* which the American studio had refused to finance because they assumed such an ostensibly "arty" film would not likely bring a profit). Pal agreed to both conditions without the least bit of reluctance.

The plot of Ladislas Fodor's script, based loosely on the Brothers Grimm story (in that all their customary emphasis on

Peter Sellers and Terry-Thomas.

brutality and horror has been removed), opens in an old forest as an aging woodcutter named Honest Jonathan (Bernard Miles) prepares to chop down a huge tree. Just as he is about to swing his ax, the Forest Queen (June Thorburn) appears and asks him to spare the tree in return for three wishes. Jonathan agrees and hurries home to tell his wife, Anna (Jessie Matthews), the good news. But they foolishly waste the wishes, and Anna is heart-broken. She hopes the Forest Queen might grant them one more wish—to give them a little boy. "I'd love him with all my heart," she says, "even if he were no bigger than my thumb."

That night they are awakened by a sound at the door. Out-side they find a tiny boy (Russ Tamblyn) only six inches tall, who introduces himself as tom and tells them he is their son. Jonathan and Anna are delighted.

After a birthday party tom is put to bed in the nursery. In the morning he is awakened by the nursery toys, which have

The wedding of Woody (Alan Young) and the Fairy Queen (June Thorburn). Bernard Miles and Jesse Matthews are at right.

magically come to life. Led by Con-Fu-Shon (voice by Dal McKennon) they welcome tom to the nursery, and soon he is singing and dancing with them.

That day Jonathan takes tom with him to the forest. On the way they are spotted by Ivan (Terry-Thomas) and Tony (Peter Sellers), two unscrupulous characters, who are amazed at the boy's tiny size. They offer to buy tom from Jonathan, but he of course brushes them off. Further on tom and Jonathan meet up with Woody (Alan Young), a likable ne'er-do-well musician. Woody is in love with the Forest Queen, but feels he must prove himself worthy of her (she is immortal, after all) before he can bestow upon her the kiss which will turn her into a mortal.

The next Sunday Woody and tom go to the fair together, where Woody has a job in the band. But Woody loses track of tom after tom tries on a pair of "talented shoes" which cause the

wearer to dance whenever music is playing, and tom ends up being carried away by a child's balloon. Ivan and Tony, who are trying to break into the town treasury, spot tom and rescue him by
shooting him down with a slingshot. Ivan then cons tom into
helping them rob the treasury by slipping through a heavy iron
grating into the treasury and tying a rope to the biggest bag of
gold. In payment they give tom one gold coin.

Later when tom returns home he is scolded by his father for
being so late. When tom is unable to sleep because he feels guilty,
Con-Fu-Shon introduces him to the Yawning Man (voice by Stan
Freberg), a toy who sings him to sleep. The next day soldiers
come to the cottage looking for the culprits who robbed the
treasury. They find tom's gold coin inside a loaf of bread into
which it had inadvertently slipped the night before when the
bread was still uncooked dough and arrest Jonathan and Anna for
the theft.

Realizing he is responsible, tom decides to find the real rob-
bers. Woody and tom discover the two villains hiding in an old
castle, dividing the gold. When Woody tries to stop them, they
knock him unconscious. Afraid they might be discovered, Ivan
and Tony grab their gold and jump on a horse to escape. But tom
hides in the horse's ear and directs the animal back to the
village — right to the town square where Jonathan and Anna are
about to be publicly whipped for their crime. Ivan and Tony are
captured, Jonathan and Anna are freed, Woody and the Forest
Queen are married, and everyone lives happily ever after.

Judging from the result, Pal would seem not to have been
terribly concerned with the areas of the film not highlighted by
special effects (and it is highly probable he found himself on very
uncertain ground with the other areas of directorial responsibility, since he had been working in such a limited and exclusively
technological field previously). But fortunately in general the
other elements seem to carry themselves. Fodor's script, though,
as shaped by Pal, is potentially something of a major liability. The
plot is very thin indeed (and thoroughly predictable, even for a
small child), and the story rather uneasily subordinated to Pal's
desire to display the special-effects artistry which took up most

of his time and the film's budget whenever possible. Not that the dialogue is without occasional witticisms, however (something which was sadly lacking in *Andersen*). Naturally, these center around the character of tom. The fact that his size (and sudden appearance on scene) is taken for granted by all (especially tom) is an effective device for eliminating inherent sentimentality in the couple's grateful acknowledgment of their having received a son (particularly memorable is tom's remark to Jonathan that he "got here as fast as I could so I wouldn't miss my birthday").

And the players' parts were on the whole well-suited to their individual comic personas (particularly Alan Young's self-consciously dolt-like Woody and Peter Sellers' and Terry-Thomas' understated and more flamboyant villains, respectively), though the Woody–Forest Queen relationship is pretty silly (notwithstanding one nice love solo by Young, "Are You a Dream," written by Peggy Lee). June Thorburn is a lovely-looking if a tad colorless Forest-Queen, and Bernard Miles and Jessie Matthews are good enough on the whole in their small roles. The songs (particularly "tom thumb's tune," a thoroughly winning theme) are all quite right also.

But the real highlight, as one would expect, are the effects sequences featuring Russ Tamblyn as tom with the Puppetoons. The 10-minute-plus nursery scene in which tom is introduced to the toys in his room would seem immensely overlong were it not for the brilliance of the result. The trick photography (masterminded by Tom Howard, who received an Oscar for it) here is astounding: everything is seen from the point of view of Tamblyn, who really appears to be six inches tall and is overwhelmed by the objects and toys around him at the same time as he performs all kinds of dazzling duets with them and scales tables, boxes and other things with effortless ease (unfortunately, though, in the scenes where tom and his human friends are together, the effects are often very obvious, particularly since Pal usually isolates tom in close-ups). That the role was no fun at all for Tamblyn (who, for obvious reasons, did not get to perform with any of his costars) certainly does not show from his nimble, extremely enthusiastic dancing and playing (it is doubtful that O'Connor would have been much better in the role). And the

Puppetoon characters designed by Wah Chang and Gene Warren—particularly Con-Fu-Shon, Jack-in-the-Box and Yawning Man, are unforgettable also.

tom thumb was barely noticed upon its release in 1958, but is well-remembered (and deservedly so) as a thoroughly charming (though decidedly more for kids than adults, who might tire of the emphasis on effects work over story) effort, Pal's best. Four years later he was to co-direct (with Henry Levin) another children's project, *The Wonderful World of the Brothers Grimm,* a compilation film composed of a few stories without much song whose impact was fatally compromised by the unwise decision to shoot it in the now-defunct three-projector Cinerama process.

Babes in Toyland

A Walt Disney Production, *released by* Buena Vista, 1961. *Director* Jack Donohue. *Screenplay* Joe Rinaldi, Ward Kimball, Lowell S. Hawley, *based on the operetta by* Victor Herbert and Glenn McDonough. *Director of Photography* Edward Colman, A.S.C. *Editor* Robert Stafford. *Art Directors* Carroll Clark, Marvin Aubrey Davis. *Set Decorations* Emile Kuri. *Costumes* Bill Thomas, Chuck Keehne, Gertrude Casey. *Music* George Bruns, *based on* Herbert's musical score. *Orchestrations* Franklyn Marks. *Libretto* Mel Leven. *Choral Arrangements* Jud Conlon. *Choreography* Tommy Mahoney. *Special Effects* Robert Mattey. *Animation Sequences* Eustice Lycett, Joshua Meador, Bill Justice, Xavier Atencio. *Makeup* Pat McNalley. *Hairstyling* Ruth Sandifer. *Sound* Robert O. Cook, Dean Thomas. *Music Editor* Evelyn Kennedy. Technicolor. Running time: 105 minutes.

Cast Ray Bolger (Barnaby), Tommy Sands (Tom Piper), Ed Wynn (The Toymaker), Annette Funicello (Mary Contrary), Henry Calvin (Gonzorgo), Gene Sheldon (Roderigo), Tommy Kirk (Grumio), Mary McCarty (Mother Goose), Kevin Corcoran (Boy Blue), Brian Corcoran (Willie Winkie), Ann Jilliann (Bo Peep), Marilee and Melanie Arnold (The Twins), Jerry Glenn (Simple Simon), John Perri (Jack-Be-Nimble), David Pinson (Bobby Shaftoe), Bryan Russell (The Little Boy), James Martin (Jack), Ilana Dowding (Jill), Bess Flowers (Villager).

Songs "I Can't Do the Sum," "Just a Toy," "Floretta," "Castle in Spain," "We Won't be Happy Till We Get It," "Lemonade," "Just a Whisper Away," "March of the Toys," "Toyland" by Victor Herbert; "The Workshop Song," "The Forest of No Return," "Slowly He Sank into the Sea" by George Bruns, Mel Leven.

With this subject, it was only a matter of time before we would stumble upon a feature from Walt Disney. Immediately a question comes to mind, one which has been posed on more than one occasion in the past: why does such an enormous gap exist between the quality of the Disney animated features (inarguably the best ever made) and that of 90 percent of his live-action outings (food for simpletons)? The answer, oddly enough, was provided by Uncle Walt himself when he said that with animation, if you didn't like you "cast," you could just tear them up. After seeing his first live-action musical, *Babes in Toyland*, I wish I could perform a similar operation on the negative.

It is certainly a shock to find oneself actually expressing hatred (a seemingly absurd word to use to describe a Disney picture — it contrasts so harshly with the personality of the man himself) toward a film which is based, after all, on a lovely Victor Herbert operetta — and which was made once before (in 1934), as everyone knows, into a wonderful low-budget Hal Roach vehicle starring Laurel and Hardy. Yet there seems to be no other way to evaluate the response which this pathetic exercise in whimsy evoked in the mind of this critic. What is most distressing of all is that, as was the case with *Hans Christian Andersen* and Goldwyn, this picture reveals all the weaknesses of its producer and none of his strengths.

The film opens in Mother Goose Village with the announcement of the impending marriage of Mary Contrary (Annette Funicello) to Tom Piper (Tommy Sands). We soon discover that the villainous Barnaby (Ray Bolger), however, has plans of his own: he fancies Mary for himself, and promptly dispatches his two bumbling henchmen, Gonzorgo (Henry Calvin) and Roderigo (Gene Sheldon), to dispose of Tom. After they make the announcement of Tom's fate to Mary ("Slowly He Sank into the Sea") — actually they are lying, since they have sold Tom to a gypsy troupe — Barnaby proceeds to woo her with talk of a "Castle in Spain" which he plans to give her should she become his bride — but Mary can think of no one but Tom. Just as she is beginning to have second thoughts (she is having grave difficulty managing the bills alone), a troupe of wandering gypsies appears in the village, one of whom miraculously turns out to be Tom. There is a joyous reconciliation, but Barnaby refuses to give up.

One day, Mary's younger brothers and sisters wander off into the Forest of No Return, and Mary and Tom go after them, ending up in Toyland, where they meet the harried Toymaker (Ed Wynn), who is concerned that he won't be able to get all the toys made in time for Christmas this year. Tom and Mary and their little group offer to help, and all looks well—until Barnaby gets word of the Toymaker's latest invention, a "poof gun" which shrinks objects to thumb size. Barnaby seizes the instrument and "poofs" Tom, sure that now nothing will stand in his way. But Tom manages to thwart Barnaby after rallying all the toys in the shop to launch a counter-attack. Soon Tom is restored to normal, Barnaby and his goons are shrunk down to size, and Tom and Mary are wed.

What could be a more appalling and insulting introductory device than having a puppet named Sylvester J. Goose (oh, how *cute!* And how clever—he even has a middle initial!) address us? Right away we know the age group Uncle Walt was aiming at this time around—five and under. The entire opening sequence is one of the most stilted and ineptly choreographed (if indeed that is the correct term) in the history of film. The perpetrator's name, according to the credits, is Tommy Mahoney, although "director" Jack Donohue (who, not surprisingly, specialized in television, and was a notorious one-take man, even on such musical vehicles as *Calamity Jane* and *Lucky Me*) should certainly share just as much if not more of the blame. With the possible exception of Robert Stevenson—whose only really respectable credit for Disney is *Mary Poppins*, and one wonders how much of the success of the picture was due to him (see next chapter), Disney didn't exactly attract the most talented directors and writers in the business for his live-action pictures (for obvious reasons—his trademark of family entertainment being foremost among them), although there were the occasional successful one-shots (Richard Fleischer on *20,000 Leagues Under the Sea* for example).

Perhaps hiring as writers for his live-action pics his producers and animators (men like Bill Walsh and Ward Kimball—who worked on the adaptation for *Babes*) was Disney's worst move, but then, surely he would never have been able to get anyone in the league of a Wilder or Sturges, Huston or Mankiewicz—or even

The Toymaker (Ed Wynn) demonstrates his latest catastrophe. Tommy Sands, Kevin Corcoran and Annette Funicello look on.

anyone as good as the versatile talents on the MGM staff, people like Noel Langley and Florence Ryerson, the scenarists of *Oz*, who worked on hundreds of films of numerous genres and types. Yet that is exactly what Disney needed most, as this picture demonstrates in every scene.

I mentioned earlier that most of the Disney live-action efforts could rightly be considered food for simpletons. This was mainly due to the fact that Disney adhered religiously to the old adage of so-called "family entertainments": "something for everyone." Unfortunately, this almost always translated into "nothing for anyone with taste." Disney never seemed to understand that the audience for his live-action features would have (or at least *should* have) expected something just as sophisticated *in its own right* in the way of entertainment as his classic animated films provided. Apparently the box-office success of *Song of the South*

Ray Bolger as the evil Barnaby.

(1946), the first feature to combine successfully live-action and animated segments, prevented him from seeing what critic Bosley Crowther remarked was that film's serious flaw: "the ratio of live to cartoon action is approximately two to one, and that is the ratio of the film's mediocrity to its charm."

Thus, the characters and situations in Disney's subsequent live-action features (beginning with *Treasure Island* in 1950—Robert Newton's performance in that film notwithstanding) were treated no differently from cartoon characters, with little dimension or personality, save what a performer (such as a Julie

Andrews or a Dick Van Dyke) could miraculously bring to them. The crucial difference here, of course, is that the "personalities" of animated characters are dictated mainly by the attention given to the myriad cells from which they are created (thus Disney's famous remark about the malleability of them), whereas in live-action one must create flesh-and-blood *characterizations* for real actors to play—actors who must be carefully chosen in order to achieve verisimilitude.

Therein lies the basic but major flaw of *Babes in Toyland*, as Leonard Maltin has astutely pointed out in his chapter on the picture in *The Disney Films:*

> There is no heart to the film. The viewer feels no emotion for any character on the screen, and when there is no empathy with a hero or heroine, a film is off to a bad start. Besides a lack of charisma on the part of the main characters, there is no menace to the villains. The whole film is played in an *opera comique* style that keeps everything at its most superficial level. Barnaby is simply not a villain; there is never any feeling of danger in any of his schemes, and the tone of the picture is such that even the supposedly scary sequence with the living trees is sugarcoated to keep it from ever getting *too* frightening. In trying to keep the film at the level of fluffy entertainment, the filmmakers forgot to breathe life into the whole production.

From the very moment the curtain rises on the horrendously theatrical Mother Goose Village set (which resembles the others in that it looks like it was pasted together from materials one would find in a dime store) one realizes that this is a stillborn, strictly cardboard enterprise. Because of Donohue's complete lack of invention (or even interest, it would seem) in staging the scenes, the settings never even come close to becoming another character in the story, as those in *Oz* do (Roy Rowland's direction in *5000 Fingers of Dr. T* makes one long for Charles Vidor; Donohue makes one long for *Rowland!*). It is as though all the actors and technical people assembled, someone yelled "action," and they all did the first thing that came into their feeble minds. There is absolutely no dimension to a single second of the picture, so therefore no interest is created in any of its elements.

Donohue and company also succeed in throwing away all of Victor Herbert's famous songs (any one of which receives better treatment on the Disneyland Records album of the film's story and score—you *know* you're in trouble when that's the case). Even "The Workshop Song," featuring Ed Wynn, which should have been the show-stopper, is abruptly and ineptly rendered in the cramped workshop set. I certainly do not share Maltin's contention that some of the numbers are "excellent"—though Annette and Tommy Sands' "Just a Toy" is at least pleasant. Their romantic duet, "Just a Whisper Away," however, is embarrassingly stiff and self-conscious, as are their "performances" in general. For some reason I always thought Annette had some acting ability—indeed she may have, though *The Mickey Mouse Club* was hardly the proper training ground for her.

Ed Wynn brings the only comic flavor or spark or life to the production—though, as Maltin says, "a little of him goes a long way." I do not agree with him that the "quasi–Laurel and Hardy act" of Henry Calvin and Gene Sheldon is "easily the funniest thing in the film" and that their rendition of "Slowly He Sank into the Sea" is a "comic gem." Both are pathetic in my view—though Calvin, impersonating Oliver Hardy, is more off-putting, since he reminds me of that most vulgar of actors, Cliff Osmond, who has mugged his hideous way through a handful of Billy Wilder productions.

One is consistently encouraged by several of the film's key elements to compare it to *Oz*, making its already major shortcomings seem all the more pronounced. Maltin mentions the talking trees in the "Forest of No Return" number. All I can say is that one prays for one of them to start pelting the achingly adorable children with apples until the little bastards are rendered senseless. Most important with regard to parallels between the two pictures, of course, is the presence of Ray Bolger. No doubt he thought it might be fun to appear in a picture again (his last had been 1953's *April in Paris*) and to be cast against type as a villain. The attempt did not work in the least—*everyone* is agreed on that. However, his broad playing contrasts badly with his beloved Scarecrow characterization, and not even the brief dance number he is given ("Castle in Spain") can begin to capture

the magic of his prancing about the Yellow Brick Road to the
tune of "If I Only Had a Brain."

Speaking of magic, not even the film's special effects can
create the requisite fascination with the story which those in *Oz*
did. Most notable, of course, is the Toyland finale, with the
wooden soldiers attacking Barnaby. As Maltin says, the sequence
is "good, although curiously not as exceptional as one would expect from Disney. It is fairly short, and the animated trickery
rather routine and not on a par with, say, George Pal's Puppetoons in *tom thumb*."

Those who agree with me that this version of *Babes in
Toyland* is a bad trip had better beware of the abysmal 1986 TV
remake, which runs an incredible two-and-one-half hours and is
directed (by Clive Donner), written (by playwright Paul Zindel)
and performed (it stars that repulsive child actress Drew Bar-
rymore) just as poorly (if not more so) as this Disney outing.

Mary Poppins

A Walt Disney Production, *released by* Buena Vista, 1964. *Coproducer* Bill Walsh. *Director* Robert Stevenson. *Screenplay* Bill Walsh, Don DaGradi, *based on the Mary Poppins books by* P.L. Travers. *Director of Photography* Edward Colman, A.S.C. *Editor* Cotton Warburton. *Art Directors* Carroll Clark, William H. Tuntke. *Set Decorations* Emile Kuri, Hal Gausman. *Costume and Design Consultant* Tony Walton. *Costume Designer* Bill Thomas. *Costumers* Chuck Keehne, Gertrude Casey. *Consultant* P.L. Travers. *Music Supervisor, Arranger, Conductor* Irwin Kostal. *Choreography* Marc Breaux, Dee Dee Wood. *Assistant Directors* Joseph L. McEveety, Paul Feiner. *Makeup* Pat McNalley. *Hairstyling* La Rue Matheron. *Sound Supervision* Robert O. Cook. *Sound Mixer* Dean Thomas. *Music Editor* Evelyn Kennedy. *Dance Accompanist* Nat Farber. *Assistant to the Conductor* James MacDonald. *Live-Action Second Unit Director* Arthur J. Vitarelli. *Animation Director* Hamilton Luske. *Animation Art Director* McLaren Stewart. *Nursery Sequence Design* Bill Justice, Xavier Atencio. *Animators* Milt Kahl, Oliver Johnson, Jr., John Lounsberry, Hal Ambro, Franklin Thomas, Ward Kimball, Eric Larson, Cliff Nordberg, Jack Boyd. *Backgrounds* Albert Dempster, Don Griffith, Art Riley, Bill Layne. *Special Effects* Peter Ellenshaw, Eustace Lycett, Robert A. Mattey. Technicolor. Running time: 139 minutes.

Cast Julie Andrews (Mary Poppins), Dick Van Dyke (Bert, Mr. Dawes, Sr.), David Tomlinson (Mr. Banks), Glynis Johns (Mrs. Banks), Ed Wynn (Uncle Albert), Hermione Baddeley (Ellen), Karen Dotrice (Jane Banks), Matthew Garber (Michael Banks), Elsa Lanchester (Katie Nanna), Arthur Treacher (Constable Jones), Reginald Owen (Admiral Boom), Reta Shaw (Mrs. Brill), Arthur Malet (Mr. Dawes, Jr.), Jane Darwell (The Bird Woman), Cyril Delevanti (Mr. Grubbs), Lester Matthews (Mr. Tomes), Clive L. Halliday (Mr. Mousley), Don Barclay (Mr. Binnacle), Marjorie Bennett (Miss Lark), Alma Lawton (Mrs. Corry), Marjorie Eaton (Miss Persimmon).

Songs "Spoonful of Sugar," "Jolly Holiday," "I Love to Laugh,"

"Chim-Chim Cheree," "Feed the Birds (Tuppence a Bag)," "Step in Time," "Stay Awake," "Sister Suffragette," "A Man Has Dreams," "The Life I Lead," "Let's Go Fly a Kite," "Fidelity Feduciary Bank," "The Perfect Nanny," "Supercalifragilisticexpialidocious" by Richard M. and Robert B. Sherman.

Twenty-five years after its release, *Mary Poppins* remains the only Disney live-action feature which can compete with his animated masterpieces, *Snow White* (1937), *Pinocchio* (1940) and *Fantasia* (1940) — and indeed, it itself contains some of the studio's most impressive work in that area. It was also for Disney the culmination of a dream which had begun with 1941's *The Reluctant Dragon:* that is, a perfect blend of live-action with cartoons and special effects such as had never before (and never has since) been reached or surpassed (not even by his own studio, as we shall see).

After Disney's first disastrous attempt at a live-action musical, *Babes in Toyland* (1961), the phenomenal *Mary Poppins,* released just three years later, would seem to have come out of nowhere. But indeed that was far from the case, as Leonard Maltin points out: "the film is really the culmination of thirty-five years' work, for no amount of enthusiasm or capability could take the place of the experience of the Disney staff, under the guidance of Walt himself, that worked together to make this film."

Maltin also observes, however, that much of the reason for the film's success derives from the fact that "Disney deliberately went out and hired "new blood" to work with his veteran staff, in what was obviously a perfect blend of veteran know-how and youthful imagination." This extended to all areas — most importantly, perhaps, to the casting. Disney must have sensed that a disservice would have been done to P.L. Travers' characters by having his standard stock company of marginal acting talents bring them to the screen. He admirably took some risks this time out, and was rewarded on every count.

Foremost among these was the casting of Julie Andrews, who had proven her singing and acting abilities in such landmark Broadway productions as *My Fair Lady* and *Camelot,* but who had absolutely no prior experience working in front of a camera.

"Jolly Holiday": Dick Van Dyke, Julie Andrews.

A similar situation was true for Dick Van Dyke and his television success with *The Dick Van Dyke Show*. He had appeared in two films prior to *Mary Poppins*—*Bye Bye Birdie* (1963), in which he reprised his stage role, and the less-than-memorable musical *What a Way to Go!* (1964)—neither of which showed him off to great advantage. Disney also employed a host of veteran British character actors, some of whom would appear in subsequent productions for his studio, but never to better advantage than here. They included David Tomlinson, Glynis Johns, Hermione Baddeley, Elsa Lanchester and Reginald Owen.

In the technical department, there were songwriters Richard M. and Robert B. Sherman, here collaborating on their first song score (they had written title tunes for a handful of earlier Disney features), and ace choreographers Marc Breaux and Dee Dee Wood, whose work Disney had seen on a recent episode of the *Jack Benny Show*—which incidentally also featured Dick Van Dyke.

"Step in Time": Van Dyke, Andrews and Matthew Garber and Karen Dotrice.

Mary Poppins begins with an aerial panoramic shot of the London skyline. Behind the credits we see Mary (Julie Andrews) sitting atop a cloud with her trademark black bag and parrot-head-topped cane, sprucing herself up. We are then abruptly introduced to Bert (Dick Van Dyke), the local one-man-band. He introduces us to the residents of Cherry Tree Lane, among them Admiral Boom (Reginald Owen), who fires his cannon at precisely the same moment every morning.

We stop at Number 17, the home of the Bankses. It seems that today marks the culmination of a series of troubles plaguing the family. Katie Nanna (Elsa Lanchester), the maid, is resigning, declaring herself unable to cope with the incorrigible Banks children. Hers is the fifth such resignation in the last month. When the children are escorted home by a local bobby after getting into yet another scrape, their father (David Tomlinson) decides that this is indeed the last straw, and proceeds to dictate

"Let's Go Fly a Kite": Glynis Johns, David Tomlinson, Garber and Dotrice.

an advertisement to his wife (Glynis Johns) detailing his criteria for the perfect nanny—in short, a strict disciplinarian. His children, Michael and Jane (Matthew Garber and Karen Dotrice), however, have ideas of their own, and present their father with their own advertisement, which he labels "rubbish," promptly tears to pieces, and deposits in the fireplace.

What no one notices is that the pieces of the letter magically fly up the chimney and come together again in the hands of Mary Poppins. The next morning, a gust of wind blows away all the old hags who have come to apply for the position, and Mary Poppins, who sails down to the Banks home via her umbrella (to the delight of the children, watching from their bedroom window), becomes the first and only candidate for the job—at least as far as she is concerned. Before Banks can even get a word in edgewise, she overpowers him with her overwhelming self-assurance, and proceeds upstairs to tend to his children. Jane and Michael are amazed by her magical powers and her ability to turn such everyday chores as tidying up into a game.

Things proceed in a practically perfect manner (to use Mary Poppins' favorite description of herself) for several weeks, during which time the children experience the time of their lives. One day while out running errands with Mary Poppins they encounter Bert, who it turns out is a friend of Mary's. Bert is practicing one of his many trades—drawing chalk pavement pictures. Suddenly, Mary asks the trio to jump into one of the paintings, whereupon they find themselves transported into the fantasy world of the picture. There Bert and Mary enjoy a brief idyll, Bert dances with some animated penguin waiters at a cafe, and the quartet boards a merry-go-round. Without warning, Mary causes the horses to leap off the platform, and soon everyone is caught up in a fox hunt, which Mary eventually wins.

Stuffy, business-minded Banks becomes incensed when his children begin relating their adventures to him. His assumption that they are not to be believed is not helped any by Mary, who, while telling their father that she never lies, nevertheless sides with him, and arranges for Jane and Michael to accompany Banks, Sr. to the bank where he works, so that they all might become better acquainted. This visit proves disastrous when the elder Mr. Dawes (Dick Van Dyke), president of the bank, snatches Michael's tuppence from him after Michael states that he was planning on giving it to the local bird woman instead of investing it. Michael grabs the money from the old man and he and Jane make a run for it. They encounter Bert in an alley. He tells them that their father means well, and that they should try to see things from his point of view. He escorts them home, whereupon he proceeds to clean out their chimney (he is working as a sweep now), giving Banks a little friendly lecture on how to compromise. Afterward, he, the children and Mary find themselves transported up through the chimney atop the roofs of the city, where Bert and his pals participate in a rousing song and dance.

Late that night, Banks is summoned to the bank and unceremoniously fired — whereupon to everyone's amazement he exclaims that he doesn't give a hoot, since he has discovered that his position has crippled his emotional life with his family. The next morning, he informs Jane and Michael that he has repaired their broken kite-flying festivities. There, Banks, informed that the elder Mr. Dawes died during the night — though happily, thanks to Banks' recitation of Mary Poppins' favorite expression, "supercalifragilisticexpialidocious," he left this life laughing. Banks is offered a promotion. Meanwhile, a saddened Mary Poppins, sensing that her work here is through, takes off toward the skies once more. Only Bert sees her leave, expressing hope that she will not stay away for long.

What should be stressed first in noting the artistic merits of *Mary Poppins* is the fact that it is perhaps the only Disney live-action feature to boast a really good *script*. Although producer Bill Walsh (who wrote many other, sickening features for the studio) is credited with the adaptation, much of the reason for the film's success in this area must be attributed to P.L. Travers, author of the original stories on which the script is based, who served as a consultant during shooting. The reader will recall that the main problems with *Hans Christian Andersen, The 5000 Fingers of Dr. T* and *Babes in Toyland* arose from ill-conceived and executed scenarios. As Howard Hawks used to say, "If it's wrong on the page, it only gets worse when it goes up on the screen" — a bit of advice that Disney could have profited from on more than one occasion. Not since the animated features of the late 30s and 40s had the term "Disneyfication" — used to describe a reworking of a famous work of literature by the studio — been applied in such a positive sense (*Treasure Island* notwithstanding).

Much of the credit for the tightness of the script can be credited to director Robert Stevenson also. No doubt Disney's having kept a close watch over the career of young British actress Hayley Mills over the previous four years made him more aware of the brilliance of the English artists. Of course necessity dictated that the cast be composed of British players, but Disney's choice of London-born Robert Stevenson to helm the undertaking was a masterstroke. Granted, Stevenson was already under contract to the studio (his other pictures for Disney included the lackluster historical drama *Johnny Tremain,* the sentimental family drama *Old Yeller,* the impressive location adventure *In Search of the Castaways,* and the ridiculous comedies *Son of Flubber* and *The Misadventures of Merlin Jones*), so one could argue that since practically no effort was involved on Walt's part to get him, his selecting him was something less than a great coup. But since we know that Disney intended this picture to be something very special, one would like to believe that in choosing the right man to tackle the project, he remembered, for example, Stevenson's splendid film version of Austen's *Jane Eyre* (1943).

One suspects that it was Stevenson's innate sense of taste and restraint (qualities common to British filmmakers like Lean, Reed and Powell which had been submerged in the many mediocre properties Stevenson had been assigned to in recent years) which kept the narrative so consistently tight (a *very* unusual quality for a Disney live-action picture) and never allowed audience attention to drop off. Particularly impressive in this regard are the scenes of pandemonium in the Banks household with the parents, the maids and the Banks children at the film's outset. One need only compare the crispness of the exchanges between David Tomlinson and Glynis Johns, with her amusing side-comments, for example, to those between Fred MacMurray and his clan in *The Happiest Millionaire* (1967, Norman Tokar), which are dull, slackly handled and more than a little embarrassing, to illustrate Stevenson's achievement here.

Although according to choreographer Dee Dee Wood, Stevenson left the responsibility for the major musical numbers in the film up to her and husband Marc Breaux, we can be certain that the major dramatic moments in the picture, with their many deft touches, can be attributed to him. Chief among these is the sequence where Mr. Banks is called to his office at night to be fired, which Leonard Maltin aptly describes as "uncommonly beautiful and haunting"; the scene toward the end where Bert and Mr. Banks confront each other for the first time and the former slyly reproves the latter for his conduct toward his children to the tune of "A Man Has Dreams"; the splendid moment (enhanced by

Irwin Kostal's wondrous background arrangements) when Banks calls the children down from their room and they discover he has mended their kite; and the dry repartee in the scenes involving the executives at the bank where Banks works.

Stevenson also no doubt had something to do with the wondrous performances of the entire cast. Most crucial in this regard was the role of Mary Poppins, which British-born Julie Andrews managed to pull off beautifully, never allowing the character to become icky-sweet or overly sentimental. That she was given an Academy Award for her role unfortunately proved to be more of a detriment than a boost to her film career, as the image of sweetness and light which she projected here and in *The Sound of Music* the following year plagued her for years afterward, forcing her to make a radical attempt to change the public's conception of her in such vulgar late '70s-early '80s fare as *10* (1979), *S.O.B.* (1981) and *Victor/Victoria*, all three of which were directed by her husband, Blake Edwards.

With reference to Andrews' costar, Dick Van Dyke, one can only quote Maltin again: "He has never had a better vehicle for his talents, which are more considerable than many TV viewers might think . . . he captures the carefree nature of Bert to perfection, with particular highlights coming in his two big dance scenes, with the cartoon penguins and with the chimney sweeps. But he also conveys a warmth and genuine friendliness that goes beyond the geniality of a good song-and-dance man. He has the rare ability to talk to children without ever talking down to them" (a quality he would again demonstrate as star of the far less successful *Chitty Chitty Bang Bang* four years later). I agree with Leslie Halliwell that his attempt at Cockney *is* lamentable, however.

Not since *Oz* have all the necessary elements of a children's picture (wit, whimsy, fantasy, sentiment) meshed so beautifully. It is certainly true, as Maltin says, that "to record every magical moment of the film on paper would be to reproduce a detailed account of the entire script."

Again, as was the case with *Oz*, it was a matter of assembling the right people in every creative department. This was certainly the most sophisticated entry in the genre since *Oz*, in terms of technical wizardry and expertise (though Disney managed to keep the costs down to a respectable $5 million, not nearly the equivalent of *Oz's* enormous $3 million budget 25 years before). Again to quote Maltin, since he really has the definitive word on the merits of the film, concerning the major sequences involving special effects:

> The whole long "Jolly Holiday" segment (approximately 25 minutes in length) is a brilliant set piece in itself. Mary and Bert stroll along through cartoon fields, stopping at a roadside barnyard where the animals join in a musical tribute to Mary. At the outdoor cafe, four busy penguins wait on the couple prompting Bert to get up and imitate their funny walk. This segues into a soft-shoe dance routine featuring Bert and the four animated penguins. Then, at the merry-go-round, when the horses break loose, Mary, Bert, Jane and Michael find themselves riding to hounds along with a host of cartoon horsemen. The finale is the animated horse race, into which our live-action friends intrude, followed by a prize ceremony when Mary wins the race.
>
> This whole sequence is filled to overflowing with fantastic detail. There is one astounding shot where we see Mary and Bert walking over a mill bridge, their images reflected in the water below; on top of this comes a family of animated ducklings, rippling through the live-action reflection! In this early part of the segment Bert presents Mary with a cartoon bouquet, which flies away in a hundred directions (it was comprised of colorful little birds); later, at the end of the horse race, a cartoon judge gives Mary a live-action bouquet, for a neat parallel.
>
> Even the transitions opening and closing the sequence are ingenious. When the foursome jumps into the sidewalk, they raise a cloud of chalk dust. At the end, when it begins to rain, the cartoon backgrounds start to blur around the live-action characters in the foreground, signaling their return to reality.

Maltin makes another important point which reminds one of *Oz:* "One of the amazing things about the film is its total stylization. Nothing in it is real; every square inch is designed, and designed with a purpose in mind." Granted, the film does occasionally seem too obviously set-bound (particularly in the scenes outside the Banks home along Cherry Tree Lane and in the opening segment, where Mary Poppins is supposed to be drifting among the clouds—this reminds one of the rather obvious celestial settings in the film version of *Carousel*, for example), as do most of Disney's live-action pictures, but most of the time the settings serve their purpose rather well. What distinguishes this film (and *Oz*) from *The 5000 Fingers of Dr. T* is that there the settings were the most attractive things in the film; here, the emphasis is on character first, so that the backgrounds become another character in the story, rather than seeming imposed on it.

Not since *Oz* has such obvious inspiration been evident in every area. Once again we have a wondrous song score. I agree with Maltin that this one marks a summit for the Sherman Brothers (although their work on *The Happiest Millionaire* runs a close second). "As good as the songs are, however, it is the delivery that puts them over," he says, and he is right: in fact, in the case of many of the numbers which do not involve special effects and where the choreographic arrangements, while not unimaginative, are not terribly elaborate (such as "The Perfect Nanny," "Sister Suffragette," "The Life I Lead" and even the Oscar-winning "Chim-Chim Cheree"), the song itself *becomes* the number.

In terms of the choreography, the big show-stopper is, of course, the "Step in Time" number with the chimney sweeps. Dee Dee Wood remembers it as being the most exciting and challenging routine she has ever experienced (although the rousing "Let's Have a Drink on It" from *Happiest Millionaire* ranks right up there also). Wood says it took more time and effort than any other single segment in the film (the "Jolly Holiday" sequence being handled mainly by the special effects department), and that it was rehearsed for weeks before the cameras rolled. It is here that all the magic which the Disney studio came to represent over the years is crystallized in a perfect mixture of dance, song, setting and special effects (the most memorable being the foursome's shooting out of the chimney portholes toward the sky and landing gently on the rooftop).

Maltin also has the last word on the film's flaws (if they could even be called that, given the avalanche of superb ingredients which dominates the entire two and one-half hours of running time):

Mary Poppins, like Mary herself, is practically perfect. It misses perfection just by a hair. Its largest flaw is overlength. While millions of children have sat in rapt attention through the whole film, few people could help but squirm at one point or another throughout the two hours and twenty minutes. Though it would be a shame to touch this film, it does seem likely that some trimming could have made it just a little bit better by sharpening its impact. Probably the easiest thing to cut would have been the whole Ed Wynn laughing sequence [which to me has always seemed an unnecessary diversion from the main storyline, inserted merely as a way of displaying another technical feat—though I suppose one could say the same thing about the "Jolly Holiday" sequence"], but this might have been retained if some judicious cutting had been done in several existing sequences. In any event the length is not fatal to *Mary Poppins;* just something that takes a bit away from its overall strength.

Another point applies more to film buffs and adults than to children. In the "Spoonful of Sugar" sequence, stop-motion live-action photography is used, and even played backward, with the children, and Mary Poppins, superimposed on top ... though the average viewer would not understand how this movie magic had been accomplished, even an untrained eye can see the graininess of the stop-action film, and the contrast of the players matted in on top.

The point is, this is the only sequence in the film where one is *aware* of special effects (except, of course, for "Jolly Holiday"). Even a trained eye is stumped for the rest of the film, and what is more, the viewer doesn't *care* how the other tricks were accomplished.

Finally, what makes *Mary Poppins* the most successful entry in the genre since *Oz* is the fact that everyone involved with the project was concerned first and foremost with making a good film and not with seeking to pander to any particular audience(s). The opposite of the old saying about pleasing people is true here: if you set out to please yourself first and trust your instincts, chances are you will end up satisfying everyone in the end. There is no better way to describe Disney's achievement with *Mary Poppins.*

Doctor Dolittle

An Arthur P. Jacobs Production, *released by* 20th Century–Fox, 1967. *Producer* Arthur P. Jacobs. *Associate Producer* Mort Abrahams. *Director* Richard Fleischer. *Screenplay* Leslie Bricusse, *based upon the Doctor Dolittle stories by* Hugh Lofting. *Director of Photography* Robert Surtees, A.S.C. *Film Editors* Samuel E. Beetley, A.C.E., Marjorie Fowler, A.C.E. *Music Scored and Conducted by* Lionel Newman, Alexander Courage. *Dance and Musical Numbers Staged by* Herbert Ross. *Art Directors* Jack Martin Smith, Ed Graves. *Production Designer* Mario Chiari. *Costume Designer* Ray Aghayan. *Set Decorations* Walter M. Scott, Stuart A. Reiss. *Special Photographic Effects* L.B. Abbott, A.S.C., Art Cruickshank, Emil Kosa, Jr., Howard Lydecker. *Music Editor* Robert Mayer. *Vocal Supervision* Ian Fraser. *Unit Production Managers* William Eckhardt, Jack Stubbs. *Assistant Director* Richard Lang. *Sound Supervision* James Corcoran, Murray Spivack. *Sound* Douglas Williams, John Myers, Bernard Freericks. *Makeup* Ben Nye. *Hairstyles* Margaret Donovan. *Animals and Birds Supplied and Trained by* Jungleland, Thousand Oaks, California. *Location Scenes Filmed in* Castle Combe, England, and Santa Lucia, British West Indies. TODD-AO. De Luxe. *Titles by* Pacific. *Title/Designed by* Don Record. Running Time: 144 minutes.

Cast Rex Harrison (Doctor John Dolittle), Samantha Eggar (Emma Fairfax), Anthony Newley (Matthew Mugg), Richard Attenborough (Albert Blossom), William Dix (Tommy Stubbins), Peter Bull (General Bellowes), Portia Nelson (Sarah Dolittle), Muriel Landers (Mrs. Blossom), Geoffrey Holder (Willie Shakespeare), Norma Varden (Lady Petherington).

Songs "My Friend the Doctor," "The Vegetarian," "Talk To the Animals," "At the Crossroads," "I've Never Seen Anything Like It," "Beautiful Things," "When I Look in Your Eyes," "Like Animals," "After Today," "Fabulous Places," "I Think I Like You," "Doctor Dolittle" music and lyrics by Leslie Bricusse.

Scenarist-songwriter Leslie Bricusse explains how *Doctor Dolittle*, which was to become one of the most costly and disastrous children's musicals in history (and also one of 20th Century–Fox's biggest flops), came about in a personal interview with this author:

> The producer Arthur P. Jacobs—APJAC, it was called, Arthur P. Jacobs Productions—brought the idea to Fox, and it was originally going to be written by Lerner and Loewe. The concept was to make it a reunion between them and Rex Harrison after *My Fair Lady*. They thought they would have assured box-office this way. So that was the concept. And Fritz Loewe retired after *Camelot* in 1961 becuase Moss Hart, the director, died, Fritz had a heart attack, and Alan Lerner had a nervous breakdown. And Fritz stayed retired until they did *The Little Prince* in 1973. So the reason I got the job was that Arthur Jacobs had wanted to make a film of a show called *Stop the World I Want to Get Off* which Anthony Newley and I were doing at that time, and in the course of our relationship I played him a score I had written about Noah's Ark, and so it was as simplistic as this: Arthur Jacobs went to Fox and said, "I've got a guy who writes songs for animals," and I backed into it literally because of the score for *Noah's Ark*. A lot of people had tried over the years to persuade the Hugh Lofting Estate to give them the screen rights to the *Dolittle* stories—I believe Disney was one of them—and were turned down. Finally, Jacobs persuaded them. I imagine it was a combination of things. First of all, Arthur Jacobs was a very persuasive fellow, because before he was a producer he was a leading P.R. man. He became a producer because he was Marilyn Monroe's P.R. man. After two or three not very successful pictures she asked him to produce a film for her about a wife with many husbands called *What a Way to Go!* Marilyn died just before it went into production, and it was finally made with Shirley MacLaine. It was Jacobs' first movie and it was successful at a time when Fox was in terrible trouble—*Cleopatra* and all those things—so he was the blue-eyed boy for a minute. Probably the same thing—which was Lerner and Loewe and Rex Harrison, who agreed to star—got it off the ground with the Lofting Estate. It was a very bizarre thing, because I came on to the project as more of a songwriter than a screenwriter, but I had always written the books—and still do—for the projects I feel I'm right for and

"My Friend the Doctor": William Dix, Anthony Newley.

Rex, bizarrely enough, wanted me as the screenwriter, not the songwriter. I didn't ask Tony Newley to collaborate on the script [as he had done with the books of their musical shows] because he was in New York in a show of ours called *The Roar of the Greasepaint* at the time. There were no restrictions from the Lofting Estate. Hugh Lofting's son, Christopher Lofting, was the one you had to get by and he was very nice, very helpful, gave me some of his father's original drawings and all sorts of things.

Bricusse's final script (which, as we shall see, was much different from his original conception) begins as we meet Matthew Mugg (Anthony Newley), an Irish cat-food seller, and Tommy Stubbins (William Dix), a local lad, in a seaport in the English village of Puddleby-on-the-Marsh, circa 1845. Discovering a wounded duck in the course of his daily rounds, Matthew tells Tommy that they should take the creature to Doctor John

Dolittle, a physician who treats animals exclusively, and who can communicate with them. We next meet Dolittle (Rex Harrison) at his opulent country home which is filled wall-to-wall with animals, such as Polynesia the Parrot and Chee-Chee the Chimpanzee. After Dolittle takes the duck under his care, Tommy asks him to relate the story of how he became an animal doctor, which he does via a flashback which shows how he became disenchanted with the human beings whom he used to treat and how, at the suggestion of Polynesia the Parrot, he decided to tend to animals exclusively, since they alone had interested him from the start. Guided by Polynesia, the doctor has mastered 500 animal dialects to date.

Dolittle is now engaged in raising money to pay for a voyage to search for the Great Pink Sea snail. When a friend sends him the rare Pushmi-Pullyu (a two-headed llama), the Doctor takes the animal to the run-down circus of Mr. Blossom (Richard Attenborough) and exhibits it for profit. He also becomes friendly with a lonely seal, Sophie, who is pining for her mate at the North Pole. Sympathetic to her plight, Dolittle dresses Sophie in a woman's shawl and bonnet and sets her free by tossing her into the English Channel. His act of mercy is misinterpreted, however, and he is arrested on a charge of murder and, although acquitted, committed to an asylum. But Matthew, Tommy and the Doctor's animal friends arrange for his escape and, accompanied by a local maiden named Emma Fairfax (Samantha Eggar), who has taken a liking to the Doctor, they all set sail to find the Great Pink Sea snail.

Following a shipwreck during a storm at sea, the adventurers find themselves on a floating island ruled by a giant native called William Shakespeare the Tenth (Geoffrey Holder). Although the newcomers are blamed for a sudden spell of chilly weather and sentenced to death, Doctor Dolittle saves the day by both curing an epidemic of colds and arranging for the giant blue whale to push the island back to its original position on the African mainland.

Then the Great Pink Sea snail arrives—also suffering from a nasty cold. Once cured by the good doctor, the grateful creature offers the inside of its spacious shell to transport everyone back

"I Think I Like You": Rex Harrison, Samantha Eggar.

to England. Dolittle, however, elects to remain behind rather than risk re-imprisonment. But after his friends have left, Sophie the Seal pays him a visit to announce that all the animals in England are on strike because of the injustices done to him and, further, that the authorities are anxious for his return. Quick to respond, Dolittle designs a saddle for the Giant Lunar Moth and soars off in the moonlight for a speedy return to Puddleby-on-the-Marsh.

Now, all of this may sound like fun, but the result, unfortunately, is a relentlessly cheerless enterprise. The problems begin with the script, but extend through virtually every major creative area of the film. Bricusse's original concept was, he says, for a very moderate-sized film, as befitting the subject: "It's a small story—a man and animals—an intimate story—it's not as extravagant as they tried to make it." Bricusse feels—and the result certainly bears out his contention—that the film was

> overly conceived as a commercial venture. There seemed to be a *tremendous* desire to spend money. Now, what I wanted to do was a small musical about the village of Puddleby on the Marsh. Fox was so besotted with the success of *The Sound of Music* that they said, "We've got to have production values, he's got to go on a voyage, it's got to be big."

Bricusse's first draft—even with the addition of the voyage—was more compact than the final version: although everything up through the episode with the courtroom trial was basically the same, Dolittle was not pronounced insane, but simply acquitted, allowing for an immediate jump to the sea voyage (thus eliminating the need for an escape plan involving the animals). Also, Emma Fairfax was not lost during the shipwreck, but instead remained with the main characters as they neared Sea Star Island. But the biggest and most important difference involved the character of an African prince named Bompo, an old friend of Dolittle's who had sought him out because he needed to find a lion to tame so that he could be named Crown Prince of his native island, Jolliginki. Bompo accompanied Dolittle, Matthew, Tommy and the animals on the voyage to Sea Star Island, providing a clear focus for the second half of the picture as all of the happenings on the island were made to revolve around this character; the merging of the two islands at the end (one of which is Jolliginki) allowed Bompo (having dueled with a lion earlier) to assume the position of King after Dolittle relinquished it, and Dolittle and company departed for Puddleby in the snail, leaving Bompo to reign on the island.

The Bompo character was in fact taken from the Lofting stories. But Bricusse was forced to write him out (substituting instead a minor character called William Shakespeare the Tenth—played by Geoffrey Holder—whom we meet once the foursome have landed on the island and who befriends them but who serves no really vital function in terms of the overall story or relations between the characters, as Bompo had) for the following reason:

> I had wanted—and could have had—Sidney Poitier for that part. And he as Prince Bompo would have been wonderful, because he was at the height of his acting career at that time. But I think Sidney was a little nervous about a caricature of an African prince since he was dealing a lot with black rights at the time. Sammy Davis wanted to do it, but Rex wouldn't hear of that. If the film had gone another way and I'd had my Prince Bompo, I could've used a super song called "I Don't Want to be a King" when Rex gets to this island, and it would have been better to see Bompo instead, because when Rex gets there, they make him honorary king, and that's a much funnier idea, and it would've been altogether better had I been able to use it. I hated all that stuff like the pink submarine, but they wanted this image, it was a terribly important thing for them. They thought it was the greatest thing that had ever happened. I thought it was a monstrous-looking thing, anyway—it reminded me of a deflated barrage, like the Goodyear Blimp had crash-landed in the Caribbean or something!

The final section of the picture is unnecessarily padded out (because it's superfluous in the first place), and threatens to stretch grimly into eternity—one can sense Bricusse's complete lack of enthusiasm for having had to abandon the elements which gave the original stories their charm (the relations between Dolittle and his animal friends) in favor of a ridiculous and totally uninteresting subplot involving the voyage to search for the snail (there is an absurdly out-of-place attempt to make up for this by the insertion during this sequence of the song "Doctor Dolittle"—Matthew describing the doctor's skills to the island children—which rightly should have been placed somewhere at the beginning of the picture—most likely in place of "My Friend the Doctor" which opens it).

Also forced upon Bricusse partly because of the prechosen presence of Harrison in the title role (in order to maintain the actor's essentially misogynist sense of humor) and also out of an

The deleted section of "Beautiful Things": Eggar and Newley inside the empty circus tent, where Eggar seems to be falling under his spell.

attempt to entice the adult audience was the inclusion of a romantic triangle involving Dolittle, Emma and Matthew (Matthew pines for Emma, but she has eyes only for the Doctor, despite the fact that he cannot relate to her). This in itself was not a bad idea at all, but it too was botched by the last-minute decision (prompted, Bricusse says, by the mutual feeling that the picture was getting too long and that there were too many ballads in the second half) to eliminate the two and a half numbers which were intended to delineate the relations between the three characters. First off was "Beautiful Things," which now appears in a truncated and highly puzzling version, as Matthew sings to Emma while the two of them twirl about on a carousel—only to have her abruptly leave seemingly in mid-song to see what Dolittle is up to. In the missing section, Matthew leads her into the empty circus tent, where she indeed seems to be falling under his spell, sharing a stanza of the song before retreating back outdoors (alert viewers will also miss the significance of her handing a baton to Matthew before leaving for Dolittle's caravan, since they did not see him hand it to her inside the tent).

The second — and one of the best moments in the film, according to Bricusse and director Richard Fleischer, who reluctantly agreed to all these cuts — came later, during the sea voyage at night. Discovering Emma asleep on a pile of clothes (she has been doing all the work on the ship, acting on the orders of Dolittle), Matthew cannot resist serenading her to the tune of "Where Are the Words." In terms of intimacy, this was undoubtedly the peak of the picture, along with one of its most colorful and diverting scenes ("I remember shooting Tony Newley's hands as he made all kind of shapes with them," Fleischer recalls excitedly).

The third (and perhaps most crucial in terms of the motivations of Dolittle — Bricusse fought hard to keep it, but to no avail), "Something in Your Smile," found Harrison sitting at his writing table one night on the island after everyone has departed for England writing in his diary a confession that he had discovered he was not as immune to human feelings as he had thought and that the possibility of a relationship between Emma and him was perhaps not an impossible thing. At the end of the song, he dozed off (in the release print, there is a dissolve from the snail departing to a shot of the island the next morning and a pan over to Harrison still at his desk, asleep). The music for "Something in Your Smile" can still be heard in the picture's overture and also, in some prints, in a three-minute post-end-credits rendition. The absence of the song makes the entire emphasis on the romantic subplot seem totally absurd — especially as Harrison departs from the island on the Giant Lunar Moth — a shot which Bosley Crowther rightly described as "embarrassing, even for children" (it also seems strange to many viewers that Emma fancies the doctor over the younger and more attractive Matthew, though Bricusse says this is because Dolittle's occupation is so fascinating to her).

It is typical of the mentality of the Fox personnel who produced *Dolittle* (recounted at length in John Gregory Dunne's excellent book *The Studio*) — headed by producer Arthur Jacobs, whose short-lived career as producer (he died in 1973) saw only a handful of successful films, namely *Planet of the Apes* (1968, directed by Franklin Schaffner), *Play It Again, Sam* (1972, directed by Herbert Ross, *Dolittle*'s choreographer) and the musical remake of *Goodbye, Mr. Chips* (1969, Ross's first feature as director, and considerably better than was thought at the time of its release)—that they would cut out virtually the only good bits in the film and leave all the rubbish.

But there are other problems with Bricusse's script which have nothing to do with the revisions and additions he was asked to make. The humor throughout is exceedingly strained and thin, amounting to little more than cute observations by Dolittle on the various animals' habits and an emphasis on silly mixed-up logic on the part of the Doctor. The Matthew Mugg character in particular is totally ludicrous and embarrassing (though Bricusse says it was Arthur Jacobs', not his, idea that Anthony Newley, whose attempt at an Irish accent can most kindly be described as juvenile, be in the picture), continually preoccupied (because of his Irish ancestry) with drinking and mooning over Emma. Also, his remarks in song to the effect that Dolittle is a fascinating man and that his world is "full of fantasy" are not borne out by the subsequent events which involve the Doctor. The introductions of Matthew ("Stop your daydreaming, Tommy Stubbins," are his first words, a lame attempt at injecting a fantastic feeling into the story, as is Tommy's "You know, if I sold my Grandfather's watch, we could build a boat and go to China") and Emma (who is singing that she is at the crossroads of her life not a minute after we've been introduced to her) are awkward and forced also, and Dolittle's first song, "The Vegetarian" (as Bricusse admits) is pretty much unnecessary (particularly in light of the flashback which follows—though the physical antics displayed in that are quite painful to watch also) and tends to grind the already unhurried pace to a halt. And, too, the misogynist motif (as will be discussed further) is misplaced.

But perhaps the most regrettable thing about the scenario of the film is the fact that so little time is devoted to the real subject: Dolittle's love for and respect of animals, which, Bricusse says, is a theme which touches old and young alike. The one piece of material which was intended to be the big moment in terms of this aspect, Dolittle's courtroom tirade against the abuse of defenseless creatures, "Like Animals," unfortunately emerged as one of the most dispirited and unharmonious numbers in the film.

With regard to the rest of Bricusse's score, he says he was embarrassed that "Talk to the Animals" (a "silly little song," in his own words) won the Oscar for Best Song; the only really good song in the film, according to him (and most viewers who see *Dolittle* today), is Dolittle's "When I Look in Your Eyes"—but, unfortunately, this was not sung by Dolittle to Emma, as one might expect, but rather by Dolittle to *Sophie the Seal!* Bricusse says his favorite projects are children's musicals, but truth to tell, his rather mediocre work on this and other efforts such as 1970's *Scrooge* (which he also scripted again) and 1971's *Willy Wonka and the Chocolate Factory* (with the exceptions of the song "Thank You Very Much" in the former and "Candy Man" and "Pure Imagination" in the latter) has unfortunately tended to obscure his reputation (at least in America; Bricusse is a native Englishman) as writer-composer (with Anthony Newley) of two of the greatest musical shows in history, *Stop the World I Want to Get Off* (which features the immortal "What Kind of Fool Am I") and *The Roar of the Greasepaint, the Smell of the Crowd*, both of which are British in origin. But at least the children's films maintain the unflagging sense of optimism and good cheer which is prevalent throughout his work: in each film, there is at least one song which extols the joy which tomorrow will bring. In *Dolittle*, it is "After Today," in *Goodbye, Mr. Chips* (1969), "Walk Through the World," *Scrooge*, "I'll Begin Again," and *Willy Wonka* "(I've Got a) Golden Ticket" and "Pure Imagination." This is perhaps the reason Sammy Davis, Jr. (whose autobiography is titled *Yes I Can*) has had such a happy and profitable association with Bricusse (and Newley) over the years.

But despite the questionable quality of Bricusse's script and lyrics (though the music by itself is lovely), the real kiss of death to the production was the appointment of Richard Fleischer as director. Fleischer had been working at Fox since 1959, and was chosen for the job because of his friendship with studio head

Richard Zanuck. Jean-Pierre Coursodon in his essay on Fleischer in *American Directors* observes that the project "seems to have put him to sleep." Coursodon also notes the very disturbing discrepancy between the downbeat trend of Fleischer's only valid early works (low-budget caper films like *The Narrow Margin*, 1952, and others concerned with "neurotic losers and loners, pitiful psychopaths locked inside their sick private worlds, the helpless and the downtrodden") and his "healthy professionalism, his cheerful willingness to tackle almost any kind of assignment." It is precisely that "cheerful willingness" which causes one to question seriously Fleischer's artistic sensibilities.

The director says now that he was "flattered by the opportunity to direct such a monumental, large scale effort — nothing like this had ever been done before, after all." The fact that he had no discernible approach to nor prior experience with the musical form did not seem to phase him in the least — the fact that he had dabbled in fantasy twice before on *Fantastic Voyage* (1966) and *20,000 Leagues Under the Sea* (1954) was negligible, since apart from spectacular special effects, both efforts remained stubbornly cardboard in their delineation of relationships among characters. Bricusse says that what was decidedly lacking in *Dolittle* was a sense of believability in the setting and characters. Because Fleischer was — and is — decidedly not an aggressive take-charge director, but rather, as Bricusse admits, a "yes-man," the fact that he succeeded in breathing not a speck of life into the production nor of succeeding in making any of the elements gel was therefore not very surprising (granted, the animals were difficult to deal with, but a good director would not let such problems stand in his way).

Fleischer states today that he cannot see what if anything is wrong with the picture, and that if he had it to do over again, he would do it exactly the same way. This might be due to an attempt to forget the myriad production difficulties which plagued him throughout the shooting (not to mention the financial debt the film incurred) and, most likely, an attempt to hide a privately acknowledged belief that he was not the right man to helm the project. But, Fleischer is completely sincere in his judgment of the film (which he recently screened again). Also related to this is his apparent sense of pride in all his films, despite their poor critical reception and or box-office success. Fleischer has helmed perhaps the longest string of costly disasters in movie history—among them *Barabbas* (1962), *Che!* (1969), *Tora! Tora! Tora!* (1970), *Mandingo* (1975), the infamous third version of *The Jazz Singer* (1980), and *Conan the Destroyer* (1984).

The only films in Fleischer's canon which are remembered with some affection besides *Fantastic Voyage* and *20,000 Leagues* are *Compulsion* (1959), *The Boston Strangler* (1968) and *Ten Rillington Place* (1971). With regard to the last two, despite some technical proficiency in creating a dark and sinister atmosphere (a skill honed in the director's early days), the films are notable mainly for their performances (Orson Welles, Bradford Dillman and Dean Stockwell in *Compulsion,* Tony Curtis in *Boston Strangler,* John Hurt in *Ten Rillington*—along with James Mason as Captain Nemo in *20,000 Leagues*). (His uncertainty as to what he wanted was what, according to Welles biographer Barbara Leaming, forced Welles to take over control of the scenes in which he appeared.)

This contention is borne out by the ensemble in *Dolittle.* Fleischer says the actors didn't get along very well, and this lack of a sense of camaraderie is certainly felt in the resulting film. The director's job is, however, to try to create a happy atmosphere among his players. Perhaps Fleischer was too intimidated by the dominating presence of Rex Harrison to try to assert himself to any great degree. Particularly upsetting is Samantha Eggar, who walks through much of the film sporting a rather sullen expression (an unintentional reminder of her performance in 1965's *The Collector,* as is the placement of a *butterfly* next to her name in the credits, something which, in light of her work in *Dolittle* and especially if one has memories of her haunting portrayal in the Wyler film, registers rather like a very sick joke, though I'm positive it was just a coincidence). One would hesitate to say that Miss Eggar was miscast, though, mainly since she eventually appears to loosen up a bit and enjoy herself, mainly toward the end. A pity indeed that Fleischer couldn't have taken her aside and instilled some confidence in her, so that numbers like "At the Crossroads," "Fabulous Places" and "I Think I Like You," would have seemed charming instead of uncomfortably self-conscious.

Bricusse says that the person who best understood the project was its choreographer, Herbert Ross. This was former dancer and TV choreographer Ross' first venture into film, and the result largely bears out John Simon's observation that his work on *Dolittle* was scant preparation for *Funny Girl* (1968), which was to follow (and in which Ross was to be saddled again with a director — William Wyler — who knew nothing about musicals). Ross' big chance was the circus sequence, but that — despite the colorful dancers and settings — turned out, despite a few moments, all involving Richard Attenborough's Blossom (including one superb closeup of the actor as he is about to descend from his caravan amid a flurry of dancing girls) — to be as limp and uninspired as in the rest of the film (Ross' best work was probably in the "Where Are the Words" number, mentioned earlier, but since it appears lost forever, we'll never know).

One irritating tendency of his (apparent in the "My Friend the Doctor" and "At the Crossroads" numbers) is to cut suddenly in the middle of a scene to a long, establishing shot of a locale, thereby dissipating whatever emotion has been created in the intimate opening moments of the number, done in full shot with the camera close to the actors. This technique surfaces again in *Funny Girl* in the "Don't Rain on My Parade" number in which Ross jumps from Barbra Streisand starting the song on a train to a helicopter shot of her on a tugboat; we do not see her in closeup again until the song is finished. And Ross' preoccupation with zoom effects and other similar technical devices in *Goodbye, Mr. Chips* all but ruins the otherwise splendid romantic aura of the songs Petula Clark and Peter O'Toole share. Also, there is in *Dolittle* a decided lack of harmony between the visuals and the orchestrations which accompany them — the latter seem to be playing against the former.

Bricusse has what would have been a truly inspired suggestion for the film: Gene Kelly. As he puts it, "Gene was a veteran of the Arthur Freed era at MGM, and the simple truth was that MGM knew how to make musicals and Fox didn't." Indeed, Kelly could have handled both the direction and choreography jobs with ease, and would undoubtedly have been able to help fix the script also.

But even with Kelly at the helm, he would still have been faced with the unsuitable presence of Rex Harrison in the title role. Ken Hughes, who directed *Chitty Chitty Bang Bang,* has perhaps the most accurate (and amusing) capsule description of the dignified thespian's presence in the title role of a man who talks to animals: "He reminded me of that old black actor Rex Ingram in *The Green Pastures* (1936), going around greeting everyone. Well, that's what Rex Harrison was doing here: 'Morning, Mr. Elephant, how's that tooth,' and 'How's our lion today.' Oh, *shit!*" (though, as Fleischer points out, an effort was made to prevent Harrison — who understandably had misgivings about accepting the role, and even walked out at one point — from being embarrassed by not having him engage in animal gibberish — that he communicates with the animals is more of an illusory principle).

As Bricusse stated at the beginning of this chapter, the project was conceived as a commercial venture resting on Harrison's participation, and so, as he puts it, "Given that it's wrong from the top, you do the best you can with the person you've got, which may not necessarily be best for what the requirements of the film are." Bricusse had no choice but to structure the songs to fit Harrison's talk-sing format à la *My Fair Lady,* since, as he says, "That's the only way Rex can perform." But Harrison further hampered the production by arrogantly insisting (inexplicably, for he had performed comfortably with the standard playback format in the film of *My Fair Lady*) that all his numbers be recorded *live,* a practice which had not been attempted since the days of the Lubitsch musicals in the early '30s. This only succeeded in further decreasing the already poor level of spontaneity in the film — as it would eight years later when Peter Bogdanovich again employed it on *his* now-infamous fiasco, *At Long Last Love* (also, coincidentally, a Fox film).

But the simple fact is that the presence of Professor Higgins (and all the misogynist humor throughout is embarrassing) is about the furthest thing from Hugh Lofting's rolly-polly creation as one could imagine ("If anything, Rex Harrison is a Harvey

Street specialist, not a country doctor, isn't he?" says Bricusse).
Although Harrison looks like he's generally having a good time
(his misgivings about taking on the part were quelled by a hefty
paycheck), he just doesn't belong here. But even more astonishing is that the filmmakers didn't have to venture beyond their
own cast list to find the man who would have been perfect in the
part: Richard Attenborough, whose seven-minute stint as
Blossom is the film's only high point, performance-wise. Attenborough plays his small role as the energetic and mercenary circus proprietor to the hilt and without a single trace of self-con-
sciousness—also, *he* bears a remarkable physical resemblance to
Lofting's Dolittle. But alas, it was not to be...

The film's other major asset is Robert Surtees' color cinematography, whose lushness keeps one watching. The special
effects, as I mentioned earlier, are largely disappointing, and the
film's other creations (such as the Pushmi-Pullyu, which is obviously two guys in a costume) only serve to betray the lack of
real imagination in the enterprise. In the end, it is probably this
aspect more than anything else which sealed the fate of the film.
Reportedly it has finally recouped its $16 million cost, but the
film itself remains, as Leonard Maltin puts it, a "colossal musical
dud." That is really all that matters.

Chitty Chitty Bang Bang

A Warfield/DFI Production, *released in the United States by* United Artists, 1968. *Producer* Albert R. Broccoli. *Director* Ken Hughes. *Screenplay* Roald Dahl and Ken Hughes, *based on a story by* Ian Fleming. *Additional Dialogue by* Richard Maibaum. *Director of Photography* Christoher Challis, B.S.C. *Second Unit Photography* Skeets Kelly. *Aerial Photography* John Jordan. *Camera Operator* John Harris. *Continuity* Angela Martelli. *Second Unit Director* Richard Taylor. *Assistant Director* Gus Agosti. *Production Designer* Ken Adam. *Art Director* Harry Pottle. *Assistant Art Directors* Bob Laing, Peter Lamont, Michael White. *Editor* John Shirley. *Special Effects* John Stears. *Potts' Inventions Created by* Rowland Emmet. *Sound* John Mitchell, Fred Hynes. *Costumes* Elizabeth Haffenden, Joan Bridge. *Wardrobe Supervisor* Jackie Cummins. *Associate Producer* Stanley Sopel. *Production Supervisor* David Middlemas. *Production Associate* Peter Hunt. *Location Manager* Frank Ernst. *Music Supervised and Conducted by* Irwin Kostal. *Musical Numbers Staged by* Marc Breaux and Dee Dee Wood. *Music Editor* Robin Clark. *Dubbing Editors* Harry Miller and Les Wiggins. Super-Panavision 70. Technicolor. Running time: 142 minutes.

Cast Dick Van Dyke (Caractacus Potts), Sally Ann Howes (Truly Scrumptious), Lionel Jeffries (Grandpa Potts), Gert Frobe (Baron Bomburst), Anna Quayle (Baroness Bomburst), Benny Hill (Toymaker), James Robertson Justice (Lord Scrumptious), Robert Helpmann (Child Catcher), Heather Ripley (Jemima Potts), Adrian Hall (Jeremy Potts), Barbara Windsor (Blonde), Davy Kaye (Admiral), Alexander Dore (First Spy), Bernard Spear (Second Spy), Stanley Unwin (Chancellor), Peter Arne (Captain of Guard), Desmond Llewellyn (Coggins), Victor Maddern (Junkman), Arthur Mullard (Big Man), Ross Parker (Chef), Gerald Champion, Felix Felton, Monti De Lyle (Ministers), Totti Truman Taylor (Duchess), Larry Taylor (Lieutenant), Max Bacon (Orchestra), Max Wall, John Heawood, Michael Darbyshire, Kenneth Maller, Gerald Taylor, Eddie Davis (Inventors).

Songs "You Two," "Toot Sweets," "Hushabye Mountain," "Me Ol'

Bam-Boo," "Chitty Chitty Bang Bang," "Truly Scrumptious," "Lovely Lonely Man," "Posh!," "Roses of Success," "Chu-Chi Face," Doll on a Music Box" music and lyrics by Richard M. and Robert B. Sherman.

Chitty Chitty Bang Bang, based on an Ian Fleming children's story, came about, not surprisingly, because of British producer Albert R. "Cubby" Broccoli, who had helmed all the Fleming-based James Bond films of the sixties. Broccoli, however, stumbled upon the story quite by accident after a scanning of his personal papers one day, not having realized that he had inadvertently acquired the rights to it when he purchased the Bond novels. His keen sense of showmanship immediately seized upon the concept of another children's superproduction which would rival Fox's *Doctor Dolittle*, then currently in production. But, as was not the case with *Dolittle*, *Chitty* was to pool the majority of its creative talent from a proven hit, namely Disney's *Mary Poppins:* promptly hired were star Dick Van Dyke (who had been longing to do another children's property ever since *Poppins* but had rejected several because of poor quality), choreographers Marc Breaux and Dee Dee Wood, the songwriting team of the Sherman Brothers, and musical conductor Irwin Kostal (Julie Andrews apparently was either not interested or tied up with other projects at the time—probably the latter—so another British leading lady, Sally Ann Howes, a former child star, was chosen).

Also unlike *Dolittle*, whose makers were primarily American, *Chitty* was to be an international production. Instead of Robert Stevenson, who had directed *Poppins*, Broccoli chose British writer-director Ken Hughes, who had tackled a prestigious production of his called *The Trials of Oscar Wilde* with much success back in 1960. Hughes selected from his repertoire the English character actors Lionel Jeffries and Anna Quayle, and also handpicked two seemingly bizarre choices: celebrated Australian choreographer/dancer Robert Helpmann *(The Red Shoes)* to play an evil "child-catcher" (to Hughes' surprise, Helpmann offered no resistance whatsoever!—he hadn't appeared in a film in quite a while) and racy British comedian Benny Hill for the role of a timid, harried toymaker.

Originally Hughes was only to direct the feature, but after receiving a first-draft screenplay from renowned children's book author Roald Dahl (Fleming had died in 1964), which he found to be unbearably icky, Broccoli handed the additional assignment over to Hughes, who came up with a workable version in some three weeks' time (he had learned to work fast from his B-picture and television days, and also from his experience on *Trials*, which had been made concurrently with another feature on Wilde; the two companies were literally racing each other, and Hughes' finally won out). He retained, however, the basic structure of Dahl's treatment, which was a complete reworking and imaginative expansion of Fleming's story. In fact, in the final analysis, the only aspects of Fleming retained were the protagonist, inventor Caractacus Potts, his two children, the focus on their magical car — dubbed Chitty Chitty Bang Bang because of the sounds it makes — the concept that Potts would have to try to sell his inventions, among them whistling candies, in order to procure the money to buy the car for his children, and the thread of an idea that the car would get the family into trouble with certain unscrupulous people who wanted to possess it. One could really say that Hughes literally discarded Fleming's story altogether, having found it unsatisfactory.

Contrary to what the critics have said, I am in agreement with him in his decision to fashion an original scenario from Fleming's basic idea. Fleming's tale to me has always seemed silly and pointless, abandoning the focus on the Pottses early on (after a none-too-exciting setup; they seem no different from any other happy family) in favor of an elongated subplot in which a group of spies abducts their prized car, prompting Potts and Co. to devise a counterattack. By contrast, Hughes came up with a cleverly constructed scenario in which the car indirectly becomes the means of strengthening a shaky family situation.

After the lengthy credits sequence, in which we are witness to the history of the racing car (it won the Grand Prix three years in a row, in 1907, 1908 and 1909), the film dissolves to a run-down garage, in whose yard two children, Jeremy (Adrian Hall) and Jemima (Heather Ripley) are playing in the remains of the

Van Dyke puts his children to bed by winding his homemade music box to play "Hushabye Mountain."

dilapidated auto (which—along with its driver—was consumed by flames after a freak explosion after the third Grand Prix victory, as we saw in the credits). It seems that Coggins (Desmond Llewellyn), the owner of the garage, plans to sell the car to a junkman (Victor Maddern), because he needs the money and because it's of no use to him anyway. The children protest, claiming that Chitty is a "special" car which has feelings just like any human. The junkman dismisses their talk as nonsense, but the kids manage to persuade Coggins to break his bargain with the junkman if they can persuade their father to give him 30 shillings (he had been offered 15 bob) for it.

"Me Ol' Bam-Boo": Van Dyke and dancers.

On the way home from Coggins' place, the children run into—literally—a local highborn maiden named Truly Scrumptious (Sally Ann Howes) when they dash out into the road and she is forced to swerve into a pond to avoid hitting them with her car. After questioning them, she discovers they have been playing truant from school, and agrees to take them home, stating that she plans to give their negligent father a stern lecture. Upon arriving at the Potts place—a collection of ramshackle buildings, one of which is a reconverted windmill—Truly is given a startling introduction to Caractacus (Dick Van Dyke) when she witnesses his latest creation—an entourage of rockets strapped to his back which he hopes will propel him skyward—backfire. Attempting to save him from almost certain obliteration, she douses him with water from a nearby well, prompting not thanks but scorn from Potts, who declares that she has ruined his propulsion unit (his suit was completely flameproof). After this unflattering first impression, Potts—a defensive widower—is all too ready to blame her for everything that has happened to his children that day, and when he learns that the tykes have missed school, replies astonishingly, "Well, it'll give the other children a chance to catch up, won't it?" A subsequent attempt by Truly to set Potts straight only provokes further hostility between them, and she departs in a huff.

Next, Potts learns of his children's deal with Coggins and, unable to tell them that he cannot afford to purchase the car (he has been careful to create and preserve an illusion of wealth and harmony among them, when in reality he has been a miserable failure as an inventor, and is very insecure as a single parent), he promises them that he will be able to "work something out somehow" with him. He first tries to sell his latest invention, whistling sweets, to Lord Scrumptious (James Robertson Justice), the owner of the local candy factory, but the demonstration turns into a catastrophe when the sound of the candies attracts dogs from all over the area, who invade the premises and destroy the candied goods therein.

Potts is forced to confess the truth about his financial situation to the children, after which they tell him to forget about their wants and offer to allow him to sell the items in their "treasure chest" (an old cog which Potts has told them used to be a crown of King Alfred, and some broken quartz crystals which he has led them to believe are diamonds) to obtain money for new inventions. Touched by their selflessness and not willing to shatter their illusions, he tells them that their offerings wouldn't be appreciated by other people, because they "don't see things the way you do" (this scene, which takes place in the children's bedroom, reminds one of a similar—though better—one in *The Trials of Oscar Wilde* between Peter Finch and his children). Now he is more determined than ever to give them the car. He brings a haircutting machine of his to the local fair, and, although he fails with that, he succeeds in securing the money by accident when, to escape from the clutches of a man whose mane he has severed, he blends in with a troupe of folk dancers and is rewarded by them for his performance. Using a few odds and ends, plus a great deal of hard work and imagination, Potts converts the old wreck into a shiny new contraption which is affectionately named Chitty Chitty Bang Bang. While on a seaside picnic with the children and Truly, Potts weaves a story about the magical powers of the car. . .

The evil Baron Bomburst of Vulgaria (Gert Frobe), spotting Chitty through a telescope from his yacht, decides he must have a duplicate of it himself, particularly after discovering that it can sail during a sea chase between the Baron and his crew and the Pottses. He sends his two spies (Alexander Dore and Bernard Spear) to abduct it, and, having failed this, they decide to kidnap Grandpa Potts (Lionel Jeffries), whom they mistake for the car's inventor. Witnessing the Baron's abduction of Grandpa by airship, Potts, Truly and the children give chase by flying in Chitty to far-off Vulgaria. There they learn that Baroness Bomburst (Anna Quayle) so despises children that she has forbidden them in the kingdom. Because of this, Jemima and Jeremy become victims of the royal Child Catcher (Robert Helpmann) and are imprisoned in the castle. Aided by the village toymaker (Benny Hill) and all the children who have escaped capture by hiding in an underground cave, Potts and Truly devise a plan to overthrow Vulgaria. Masquerading as life-sized puppets, they gain entry to the Baron's birthday party. At a given signal, all the children rush in and lead a successful mutiny in freeing Vulgaria from tyranny. With Grandpa, Jemima and Jeremy rescued, all fly back to England in Chitty. . .

Back at the beach, we realize this has indeed all been one of Potts' stories, despite the fact that it seemed real at the time. The children draw their own conclusion to the tale by adding that Potts and Truly (who have vicariously grown closer through their collaboration in the story) should get married, a suggestion that Truly willingly responds to, but which embarrasses Potts, who feels he is still a failure. Truly is angered by his inability to believe in himself, and departs, leaving the trio uncertain as to whether they will see her again. Arriving home, they discover that Lord Scrumptious has been spending the afternoon with Grandpa (the elder man, it turns out, had been Grandpa's brigadier), and has become convinced that Potts' whistling candies would be excellent treats for dogs. He offers Potts a multi-

The final scene.

million dollar contract. But before he can sign, Potts rushes off to tell Truly, who herself has already been informed (she is Lord Scrumptious' daughter). They decide to marry after all, as Potts declares that from now on he will "keep his feet firmly on the ground," not realizing that his car, meanwhile, has taken to the skies once more.

After *tom thumb* and *Babes in Toyland, Chitty Chitty Bang Bang* remains the only film discussed thus far which did not consciously strive for an adult appeal (as we just saw in the case of

Truly (Howes) and Potts (Van Dyke) comfort a homeless boy with a chorus of "Hushabye Mountain" in the cave underneath the castle.

Dolittle, such an attempt could prove particularly embarrassing when it seemed forced)—although writer-director Hughes says he deliberately "ignored Broccoli's mandate to keep the piece at the children-wildren level—about age 4—and tried to raise it to at least 12." As such the film deserves credit for its lack of pretension in acknowledging its audience and for not trying to stray from it.

Neither did Hughes, who was used to dealing exclusively with adult-oriented fare, condescend one bit in his approach to the material. The relationship between Potts and his two children, as well as that between Truly and the trio later on, generates a great deal of warmth and good feeling (its spirit was best characterized by *New York Times* critic Renata Adler in her review—one of the few to explore in any depth this side of the film—in her statement that the movie exudes "something of the joys of singing together on a team bus on the way to a game")—a

quality which was sadly lacking in *Dolittle.* No doubt a result of
the fact that Hughes loves children in real life. Hughes manages
to get away with several potentially banal exchanges precisely
because of what Adler describes as his "subtle, intelligent con-
cessions to a child's view of the absolute, unappealable ar-
bitrariness of adult power." She cites Potts' habit of responding
to crucial questions with a simple "Well, we'll see." There is also
one neat line spoken by Jemima early on while she and Jeremy
spy on Potts and Truly at the beach: "As soon as he kisses her,
then they'll *hafta* get married"—which is echoed by Truly herself
at the film's climax. There are other brief but deft *visual* touches
also, such as when Potts, distraught at not being able to find a
method for procuring the car, leans against a fence staring at a
caravan in the distance and, as he begins to formulate a plan for
using the carnival to his advantage, the music heard in the distance becomes louder and louder, finally reaching a climax as the
camera moves in for a closeup just as he's made his decision.

Perhaps the most pleasing thing about *Chitty* as compared
to *Dolittle* is that here the result—for better or worse—is really
one man's vision, more or less: Hughes took the assignment
firmly under his wing and did the best he could with it, whereas
on *Dolittle,* as we saw, there seemed to be little if any com-
patibility between Bricusse's script and Fleischer's handling of it.
And, in general the picture is excellently constructed—there
isn't really much evidence of unnecessary plot gimmicks invented just for the sake of adding to the running time, as had
been the case with *Dolittle.* Particularly admirable is the way
Potts and Truly are thrown together by chance circumstance at
the beginning, and her subsequent participation in helping vin-
dicate him as both an inventor and a man. There is a nice subtle
hint that Truly and the Pottses share some kind of spiritual affin-
ity when she instinctively thinks up her own choruses of two
songs which "belong" in a sense to the Pottses, "Chitty Chitty
Bang Bang" (sung while the foursome ride to the seaside) and a
reprise of Potts' lullabye "Hushabye Mountain" which she and
the professor sing to comfort the forbidden children. This last
scene—in which Potts, Truly, and the toymaker descend by row-
boat underneath the castle to query the miserable, wretched

youngsters about the whereabouts of Jeremy and Jemima—
quivers with feeling, and is Hughes' best creation—though the
original concept of a land where children are forbidden was
Dahl's.

Unfortunately, however, in most other respects—and even
to an extent in the ones just mentioned—Hughes' handling of the
subject matter in terms of writing and direction can be faulted.
His main problems are that as a writer he is unavoidably
pedestrian and as a director he lacks a firm control over the
elements in a scene. (This is not really the result of his tackling
unfamiliar ground either, since the same can also be said of his
hopelessly schoolbook-level historical epic of two years later,
Cromwell, for example, as well as the great majority of his films
as writer-director, with the exception of *The Trials of Oscar
Wilde*.) One would be hard-pressed to find one really strong
scene in the picture, one that was not compromised in some way
by the director's uncertainty. As Pauline Kael commented, "One
gets the feeling that all concerned were trying to do their damnd-
est, but that everything somehow went hopelessly wrong" (*Kiss
Kiss Bang Bang*, p. 50). To Hughes' credit, though, he *does*
possess an excellent visual-narrative sense: he always knows exactly where to put the camera, if little else (this couldn't be said
of very many of the other directors discussed thus far). This is
what helps sustain interest throughout, however much one may
become uncomfortable with the characters and approach, and
keeps the picture accelerating along (something which *Dolittle*
didn't do at all).

A big problem is that most of the characters are either im-
precisely delineated, insufficiently developed, or grossly overdrawn. The picture reeks with eccentrics, none of whom are
anything more than pale copies from previous pictures.
Hughes—who created such characters as the bizarre Grandpa
Potts, who spouts ancient vaudeville jokes like the one about the
elephant in my pajamas and has delusions that his privy doubles
for countless adventure locations—says this is just "typical
English humor which comes from my Monty Python–type
background." Maybe so, but it is much more tiresome than funny.
Particularly offensive are the two spies played by Alexander Dore

and Bernard Spear, who perpetrate some of the most badly timed physical antics ever put on film. Hughes says Dore is an old friend of his who "could have been another Danny Kaye if he'd been given the right break": given the evidence of this film, one finds it extremely difficult to agree with him.

The other attempts at physical comedy — such as the Baron's wife being accidentally shot into the air by a faulty spring in the car where she is sitting and his gleefully shooting her down — are also nothing we haven't seen a thousand times before. Also negligible are the characters of the Baron and the Child Catcher, to whom Hughes gives all the predictable wicked lines, such as "I will cut off your head and feed it to the dogs" (by contrast, he neglects the Baron's wife, who seems to be the most interesting character in this segment: Anna Quayle, who, Hughes says, "liked to do bizarre things," seemed to bring something playfully sinister to her part). Hughes justifies this by explaining that "details have to be made very clear for children. A villian is a villain. He wears a black hat and kicks a dog." Maybe so, but one finds the same sort of tired rehashing of cliches in other films written and directed by Hughes, such as the Bluebeardesque black comedy *Drop Dead Darling* (1966). There also seems to be some would-be political satire in the Vulgaria episode, but as Pauline Kael pointed out, this was hardly the place for it (Hughes says that it is an "instinctive British trait to make fun of Germans").

There are also logical errors which stand out, such as the fact that Potts' two children unaccountably sport English accents, while their father is American. Hughes says now the thought never even crossed his mind — all he knew was that he was determined that Van Dyke not attempt the pitiful English accent he had employed in *Mary Poppins*. In addition, the final implication that the whole Vulgaria episode may have indeed happened — a standard, "classic" device, as Hughes himself admits — is questionable because if indeed that were the case, when the trio landed back on the beach in England, Grandpa, who departed Vulgaria with them, would have to have been in the car also, and he was not. Also, the second-to-last scene — in which we discover that Grandpa and Lord Scrumptious have been entertaining each other all afternoon — does not make sense in this context. Hughes says that this abrupt turnaround (not five minutes after Truly has left Potts presumably forever, they agree to get married) is excusable in this context, but "if this had been a serious film like *Cromwell*, I would've said, 'You've got to be joking'." And he is right in this respect.

In terms of the elements of the story, as Leslie Halliwell points out, they don't really gel, but instead are given "equal shares of the limelight." And despite the fact that Hughes basically manages to keep one watching, the picture never really achieves the true spark of energy and imagination necessary to transport an audience. Hughes says the film would've had more spontaneity if he and his crew and cast had been pressed for time; the production dragged on for a year. It is doubtful that a shorter shooting schedule would have helped much though — as it did, for example, on *The Trials of Oscar Wilde* — because the basic problems with the piece lay in the material itself.

Of course, a big problem is the horrendous process work — some of the shoddiest special effects ever, particularly the shots of the foursome steering to escape from the Baron's guns in the car on the water (why couldn't they have been towed around in the floating car — there are aerial shots of the car in the water anyway?) and the unforgivably bad moment where the car is forced to "fly" down a mountain — this spoils the final shot also, incidentally. Hughes says the effects as conceived were fine, but that a technician in the Technicolor lab (not John Stears, who simply set up the machines that created the effects) mucked them up. A pity, particularly in such an expensive production — and in a fantasy story which depends on these key moments for credibility.

Hughes also is not terribly good with actors — though he has managed to preserve an atmosphere of comradeship; no one looks uncomfortable or embarrassed here, as had been the case on *Dolittle* ("At least we had a bit of fun once in a while, despite all the difficulties in the production," Hughes says, comparing the making of *Chitty* to that of *Dolittle*). Van Dyke is appealing, and exudes a gentle nuttiness, but little else (though he gives it his all in terms of dancing in two difficult numbers, "Me Ol' Bam-Boo" and "Doll on a Music Box"): he hasn't the flair here which illuminated his Bert in *Poppins* — not that his performance in that film had much to do with his director, Stevenson, though; it was just a better conceived part. Pauline Kael had something when she said Van Dyke seemed at 43 too young to be saddled in this type of doting father characterization; sadly, though, Van Dyke has been offered very few opportunities in film since to capitalize upon his unique comedic and dramatic skills, and his sixties work has come to be considered the capstone of his career.

Sally Ann Howes's part requires her to be little more than a chocolate box princess (one suspects that Julie Andrews — at her peak of screen popularity at this time — wouldn't have been interested in playing second-fiddle) — though a ravishing one, especially when one considers that she was Van Dyke's age at this time. She tends to come on too strong in her early scenes with Van Dyke — as does he with her — a factor which makes one decidedly uncomfortable (Hughes was aiming for a kind of sophisticated cat-and-mouse kind of verbal sparring, but the result comes off as silly and juvenile) and which could have been corrected by a sharper directorial hand than Hughes', since both are excellent performers generally — though Howes' screen appearances also have been infrequent, even more so than her costar's. Of the two children, the little boy, Adrian Hall, is dreadful, but eight-year-old Heather Ripley is a very smart, instinctive actress (even Kael conceded that she was "adorable"). The less said about Lionel Jeffries' Grandpa, James Robertson Justice's Lord Scrumptious and Gert Frobe's Baron, the better — though the always commendable Robert Helpmann, despite his average material, endows his child catcher with something profoundly disturbing — friends of mine who are in their 20s are still frightened by him whenever they catch the film on TV or in revival!

With regard to Broccoli's decision to produce a film which would rival *Mary Poppins,* several things must be said. First, according to Hughes, the Disney film was never discussed on the set, because "the concept was entirely different." That is unfortunate, because had that been the case, a better film might have resulted. But parallels become inevitable when one looks at the numbers choreographed by Marc Breaux and Dee Dee Wood, who had worked on *Poppins* also. There definitely seems to have

Director Ken Hughes (kneeling) checks angle of trap door through which Anna Quayle as the Baroness will drop in "Chu-Chi Face" number.

been an attempt on their part to outdo their work on the earlier film — and, indeed, by contrast to *Poppins, Chitty* features not one but several elaborate numbers. But excellent and imaginative and diverting though they often are, they somehow can't equal the socko bits in the earlier film. The "Me Ol' Bam-Boo" dance routine between Van Dyke and the dancers at the county fair is cleverly integrated into the story—Potts becomes more and more adept at the dancing routines as he goes along—and involves some complicated legwork, but it does not generate the electricity which the "Step in Time" routine in *Poppins* (which it is trying to surpass) did.

The "Toot Sweets" number in the factory, with the exception of a few moments when Van Dyke and the workers kick up their heels atop a platform or when he and Howes jump aboard a candy cart and twirl around the room, is cinematically disappointing also—especially considering that it took three weeks to shoot (partly because Van Dyke sprained his ankle in rehearsal)—Hughes says a third of it ended up on the cutting room floor, and if one looks closely, he can see what was taken out.

"Lovely Lonely Man," which Howes sings after Van Dyke drops her off at the foot of her mansion one afternoon, is itself quite beguiling—though Hughes almost destroys the mood created by the lead-in music by cutting away to a shot of the two spies looking after the departing car. Howes in white frilled dress saunters breathlessly across the elegant manicured lawn, stopping to feel the spray of a fountain (to which the camera gets so close one can hear the water cascading), and skipping across the stones on a small lake (one recalls Samantha Eggar in *Dolittle* and now realizes just how much warmth she lacked there). The number ends with a beautiful high-angle shot of her running away from camera toward the mansion. It is one of those rare moments which takes one's breath away. Hughes appropriately concludes with a fade-out.

The other two set-pieces of note (the ones which are the most adult-oriented) are the vicious "Chu-Chi Face" patty-cake dance routine performed by Frobe and Quayle, and the deliciously inventive "Doll on a Music Box," with Howes and Van Dyke. In the first, the Baron serenades his wife on the morning of his birthday, all the while laying more and more obvious traps to do her in—which she somehow always manages to avoid. There is a marvelous surprise at the end after she falls through a trap door he has set up, only to dash his hopes by reemerging, miraculously unscathed, through a side door. In the latter, the two stars, dressed as dolls, sing while confining themselves to the creaky movements of marionettes—and their routine has an underlying significance as it becomes a declaration of Potts' love for Truly; at the end, however, she pulls her hand away just as he is about to kiss it, since she is not yet convinced that he really believes himself worthy of her.

Despite the frequent excellence of the routines, nearly all of them are played to bottom-drawer songs by the Sherman Brothers, some of which are downright ridiculous (Grandpa's "Posh!" and "Roses of Success") or unbearably stiff and sugary ("Truly Scrumptious"). The title tune was their attempt to equal "Supercalifragilistic," and though superficially clever like "Talk to the Animals" in *Dolittle*, it too has unfortunately far surpassed in popularity the one good song in the picture ("Hushabye Mountain," which was recorded by no less estimable an artist than Tony Bennett). The problem with most are their too-pat rhyme schemes (but then, most forgettable tunes have this problem). Irwin Kostal's arrangements, though, are excellent, capitalizing on the quite pleasant musical motifs which don't sound half as bad without the words attached.

Veteran production designer Ken Adam gave the production a "surrealistic, theatrical look," says Hughes, and indeed most of Adam's artistry can be glimpsed in the numbers previously mentioned. Hughes says that the choice of Rowland Emmet to create the many Rube Goldberg–like inventions (which are quite ingenious) in Potts' laboratory and home was an unnecessary publicity gimmick on Broccoli's part. And one must also mention Christopher Challis' color photography, often stunning (as in a long shot of Van Dyke walking away from camera toward a sunset, or in the "Lovely Lonely Man" number), and not usually glossy for its own sake.

All in all, *Chitty* remains a slightly better film than *Dolittle* — not really out-and-out bad, just not very good. Happily, this time one did not get the impression of money having been lavished unnecessarily — the production cost about $8 million, and managed to just recoup its cost. Before closing I should like to talk a bit more about Ken Hughes, whose greatest financial success *Chitty* proved to be. Although he had always been popular in his native England, in the late '70s — due to decreasing returns from unprofitable pictures, no doubt (taxes are notoriously high in and around London), he was forced to move to the

United States, where he found himself a stranger, his pictures never having received a very warm reception here. Since then his movie career has ebbed to nothing, the result of such bombs as *Sextette* (1978), with 86-year-old Mae West strutting her stuff for the last time, and his last to date, the abysmal teen slasher thriller *Night School* (1981) — a highly surprising offering from the director of the innocent *Chitty*. The fate which has befallen Hughes (67 years old in 1989) is unfortunate, since he is much more deserving of success than someone like Richard Fleischer — who has managed to thrive on a series of fairly expensive (though terrible) features of late — since Hughes has absolutely no pretensions about his work, and is able to acknowledge his mistakes and shortcomings. His best and favorite film remains *The Trials of Oscar Wilde*, though if he is remembered for anything at all, it will probably, for better or worse — at least in the minds of most — be for his only famous feature — at least in the United States — *Chitty Chitty Bang Bang.*

Pufnstuf

A Sid & Marty Krofft Production, *released by* Universal Pictures, 1970. *Producer* Si Rose. *Executive Producers* Sid & Marty Krofft. *Associate Producer* Malcolm Alper. *Director* Hollingsworth Morse. *Screenplay* John Fenton Murray, Si Rose. *Director of Photography* Kenneth Peach, A.S.C. *Camera Operator* Kenneth Peach, Jr. *Assistant Cameramen* John Greer, William McGovern. *Art Directors* Alexander Golitzen, Walter Scott Herndon, Joe Alves. *Set Decorator* Arthur Parker. *Film Editor* David Rawlins. *Assistant Editor* Skip Greene. *Music Composed and Conducted by* Charles Fox. *Choreography* Paul Godkin. *Sound Mixers* Walden O. Wilson, David H. Moriarty. *Assistant Sound Mixers* Don Bolger, Ed Somers, Jr. *Assistant Directors* Chuck Colean, Warren Smith. *Production Manager* Joseph Kenny. *Assistant to the Producer* Trudy Bennett. *Production Coordinator* Don Ramsey. *Script Supervisors* Dee Cooper, DaLonne Jackson. *Men's Wardrobe* Ken Harvey. *Women's Wardrobe* Barbara Harootunia. *Makeup* Bud Westmore, Ziggy Geike. *Special Effects* Luke Tillman, Roland Chiniquy. *Puppet Creation* Rolf Roediger, Evenda Leeper, Troy Barrett. *Gaffer* Lloyd Peter. *Props* Sol Martino, John Faltis. *Casting* Harold Rossmor. *Dialogue Coach* Dale Ross. *Hairstylist* Larry Germain. *Costume Supervisor* Vincent Dee. Technicolor. Running time: 98 minutes.

Cast Jack Wild (Jimmy), Billie Hayes (Witchiepoo), Martha Raye (Boss Witch), Mama Cass (Witch Hazel), Roberto Gamonet (H.R. Pufnstuf), Sharon Baird (Shirley Pufnstuf), Johnny Silver (Dr. Blinkey), Andrew Ratoucheff (Alarm Clock), Billy Barty (Googy Gopher), Felix Silla (Polkadotted Horse), Jane Dulo, Jan Davis, Princess Livingston, Joy Campbell, Angelo Rossito, Van Snowden, Lou Wagner, Hommy Stewart, Pat Lytell, Buddy Douglas, Jon Linton, Bob Howland, Scutter McKay, Roberta Keith, Penny Krompier, Brooks Hunnicutt, Barrie Duffus, Evelyn Dutton, Tony Barro, Ken Creel, Fred Curt, Dennis Edenfield, Allison McKay.

Songs "If I Could," "Fire in the Castle," "Living Island," "Witchiepoo's Lament," "Angel Raid," "A Friend in You," "How Lucky I Am,"

"Living Island" number.

"Pufnstuf," "Charge," "Different," "Zap the World," "Leaving Living Island," "Rescue Racer to the Rescue," music and lyrics by Charles Fox and Norman Gimbel.

Few realize that there exists a motion picture derived from the popular kidvid series of 1969–70, *H.R. Pufnstuf*—and never was the phrase "ignorance is bliss" more welcome. According to Si Rose, who produced and wrote both the TV program and the film, everyone connected with the venture (in particular the executives at Universal, the film's distributor) believed they had the makings of the biggest box-office hit of all time. And you thought the old Hollywood moguls were reprehensible in *their* gross underestimation of the intelligence of the American public.

This movie (and the TV show which spawned it) was the creation of producers Sid and Marty Krofft, the team responsible for a slew of Saturday-morning offerings of questionable taste in the early '70s. Their idea was to create a sort of variation on *Oz*,

with a male protagonist, feeling alienated from his home surroundings, escaping to a fantasy land peopled by strange but
friendly creatures. Unfortunately, the similarities end there.

It seems pointless to describe or critique a film which is so
sadly lacking in any semblance of intelligence whatsoever (indeed, it is not even a noble failure, like some of the others listed
herein); the best way to show how truly inferior the enterprise
is to compare it to its obvious model, *Oz* (this is the only film in
the book which demands such a close comparison, not because
of quality, but only by virtue of basic concept and storyline).

We are clued in to the anticipated age level of the audience
from the first seconds of the picture: before the credits, "Witchiepoo" (Billie Hayes) rushes, growling, into a black frame from off
camera and orders the viewers to "Sit down and be quiet while
I tell you a story that's going to tear your hearts out. It's about a
gang of goody-two-shoes—just like all of you out there—and
what they did to poor, sweet, adorable me." As we hear the sound
of a boy saying goodbye to his parents, she continues, "You hear
that? That's the rotten kid that started it all. Let me show you
what happened. And don't go away, or I'll zap you all into little
frogs." She then lifts the frame above her head, and the screen
is enveloped by a helicopter shot of a suburban community.

We next see little Jimmy (Jack Wild) leaving his country
home for school, flute in hand. The credits are superimposed
over a rather crude montage of shots of Jimmy frolicking about
the countryside (it is composed, as is much of the rest of the film,
of unnecessary and repetitious cut-ins and cut-outs and zoom
effects, presumably used to lengthen the sequence to fit the song
over the credits, "If I Could").

As the last credit appears, he realizes he has been dawdling,
and rushes off to Elmhurst Junior High School, where the band
of which he is a member is in the middle of practice. As he rushes
to take his place, one of the boys trips him, and he falls head first
into a drum. The others, who resent Jimmy because of his English accent and background, blame *him* for causing the incident,
and the pea-brained bandleader is all-too-quick to side with
them. Jimmy is banished from the band.

Top: *Jimmy (Jack Wild) trapped in boat which will take him to Living Island.* Bottom: *Jimmy organizes a plan to get Pufnstuf out of the Witch's castle.*

Trudging through a nearby forest, he stops to rest by a tree, discarding his flute nearby — at which point it goes through an inexplicable metamorphosis after which it becomes not only solid gold but also sports a voice! Jimmy, astounded, comments, "I never heard of a flute talking," to which the flute, named Freddy, replies, "Did you ever speak to one before?" — an all-too-obvious attempt to recapture the clever repartee between Dorothy and her friends in *Oz*.

Grateful for some companionship, Jimmy skips merrily through the countryside, singing "A Friend in You" while Freddy provides musical accompaniment. At the foot of a hill they happen upon a talking boat from a place called Living Island. Another, more lame exchange: Jimmy: "Freddy, that boat spoke to us." Freddy: "Well, let's not be rude to him." Jimmy: "Of course not. Some of my best friends are boats." They hop aboard, and enjoy the temporary escape from the drudgeries of school — until Witchiepoo (Billie Hayes), riding her broom in the sky, spots Freddy and decides that having a solid gold flute in her possession would make her a shoe-in for Witch of the Year at the upcoming Witches Convention. Waving her wand, she causes the boat to sprout hands, which grab Jimmy, and orders it to take them to her castle. But Jimmy escapes and dives overboard.

Meanwhile, on nearby Living Island, the mayor, a dragon named H.R. Pufnstuf (Roberto Gamonet), spots the boy in trouble through his telescope, and orchestrates a rescue party to save him. Witchiepoo is foiled, but vows to get possession of the flute one way or another. Jimmy is then introduced to the inhabitants of the island, animals, plants and inanimate objects which are all able to speak. The remaining details of the plot are too depressing to get into: suffice it to say that they consist entirely of many redundant attempts by Witchiepoo to get possession of Freddy, and subsequent schemes by Jimmy, Pufnstuf et al. to rescue the flute, which they eventually do, and also themselves.

For those who are not familiar with the television program of the same name (but then, why would any such person want to see this film?), the title *Pufnstuf* initially arouses some interest, simply because of its absurdity: who or what *is* Pufnstuf, one asks (the same holds true, though to a lesser extent, for Witchiepoo's invitation — actually a threat — to stay and hear about the events that brought about her downfall). Unfortunately, because the exposition (not to mention the rest of the picture) is so juvenilely put over, we are not made to care about the subsequent answers.

Unlike in *Oz*, we do not get to really know Jimmy before he journeys (literally, in this case, for he is not hallucinating) to his fantasy land; we are not given even a glimpse of his family, however dull and unsatisfying they may be (though one would suspect that if Jimmy felt close to anyone at all, it would be to them, presumably the only other Britishers around). His alienation from his surroundings is summed up all too briefly (and with a maximum of callousness) when one of the kids at band practice advises him to "go back to jolly old England."

What is even more distressing is that there is very little logic to these opening scenes: there is no explanation for Freddy's sudden change, nor for the appearance of a talking boat out of the blue. In *Oz*, fantasy and reality were clearly separated, with all the magical happenings taking place in the dreamlike kingdom of Oz (there is no reason to believe the forest Jimmy enters is anything out of the ordinary, and he is certainly not conjuring it up in his mind).

It is hard to muster up concern for Jimmy's plight when he is plunged headlong into a fantastic world only seconds (or so it seems) after his home situation has been (unsatisfyingly) established. Furthermore, the place where he eventually finds himself, Living Island, seems only a stone's throw from his home turf, since no dissolves are used during his all too brief boat ride (also, one would assume he wouldn't be able to swim more than a few miles before he became tired).

The rest of the film is characterized by a general lack of direction and a pandering to the minds of the lowest types who could possibly afford the price of a theater ticket. By contrast to Dorothy, Jimmy is not really on a journey headed toward some specific goal; rather, he concerns himself mainly with rescuing Freddy again and again when he is kidnapped by Witchiepoo, and only incidentally does the thought of his getting off the island come up — only to be abandoned at the rather hasty climax, when

Jimmy apparently decides to remain there "happily ever after," as scenarist Si Rose so uniquely puts it. Why then even dwell on the subject at all, since going home had not been a goal of Jimmy's from the start, as it *had* been with Dorothy?

Of course, there is no character development either—just an endless (the running time of this feature is an incredible 98 minutes!) plethora of situations involving characters frantically chasing and or jumping about, ramming into objects, or being batted on the head. Those characters that do appear are infantilely conceived (a detached skull that does a Boris Karloff imitation, and others which mimic—pathetically—Robinson, Bogart and Ed Wynn).

Despite the obviously limited appeal of the endeavor, Si Rose maintains that he and John Fenton Murray, his co-author, along with the Brothers Krofft, intended the film (and the TV show) to appeal to both the adult and child simultaneously, in the *Oz* tradition. Specifically Rose says that the character Witchiepoo would presumably come off as "frightening to small children but amusing to adults because she is so cartoonlike and overdrawn." What made Margaret Hamilton's famous characterization so memorable is that she played it realistically, instead of as a caricature, thereby ensuring believability in both instances. The ludicrous Billie Hayes (whose screech is so irritating that one wishes for accidental de-voicing or at least a muzzle), on the other hand, does not really succeed in either department—but especially not in the latter.

What is perhaps most laughable about the script and story end of the project is the following statement by the Kroffts which appears on the back jacket of the soundtrack album for the film: "To the young, *Pufnstuf* is a *Wizard of Oz*-like fantasy, but for the very sophisticated and old, it is a highly polished satirical farce, poking fun at some of our more sacred institutions." Of course, just what those institutions might be are not examined in any detail; in fact, they cite the witches in the story as being "central to this theme."

Just what basis in reality do such characters as Witchiepoo and Boss Witch (Martha Raye) have? *Pufnstuf* can be considered a sophisticated satire about as much as *The Dukes of Hazzard* (a show not coincidentally *also* written and produced by Si Rose!) can be termed a hard-hitting exposé of Southern manners and morals. It does *unintentionally* satirize one particular aspect of American society: the TV-educated generation, which the Kroffts have produced countless shows for.

Turning to other aspects, the direction of the late Hollingsworth Morse (who also served in the same capacity on the TV program) is beyond primitive. There is not even an elementary grasp of point of view/camera placement, let alone a temperament or visible approach to the story or characters (again, Morse was TV-trained). Compared to Morse, Charles Vidor is Ernst Lubitsch and Jack Donohue, William Wyler. What is most distressing is that Morse's being an elderly British gentleman disproves my theory about older directors having an edge over younger ones in handling these types of subjects.

The scenario needs no further comment, except to note that there is no real charm (despite a sustained amiability) to any of the enterprise—but then, actors are largely responsible for creating this also, and without material, what can they do? Child star and teen idol Jack Wild may have achieved temporary stardom by hooking up with the Kroffts, but he only succeeded in doing his career in. It is sad to see the talented young man who received a Best Supporting Actor Oscar nomination in 1969 for his role as the Artful Dodger in *Oliver!* saddled in this type of nonsense. He does his professional best, though, never condescending to the material (though he had every reason to), and shows occasional sparkle, but there is no denying he was wasted here. According to Si Rose, Wild's career as an actor ended soon after this, partly the result of his shortness and too-boyish looks (he was 18 at this time, playing 11 or 12!), and he returned to his native England to become an agent. It is even more pathetic to see the wonderful Martha Raye trapped in this film. But the late Mama Cass, however, playing another witch, somehow manages to stand out hilariously, as if she were in an entirely different film, with a much sharper writer and director assigned to her. She has a brief funny bit of gossip with another witch about a third's romance with a prince whom she turned into a toad, but the affair ended with her giving him warts. Cass also has the only good song in the picture, "Different," which taken straight has the sound of a commercially successful rock lament about individuality, but done in story context by a buzzard-beaked witch takes on a comical double meaning. The other undistinguished tunes are by Charles Fox and Norman Gimbel, who have written mainly TV themes.

The work of veteran production designer Alexander Golitzen, a Universal contractee, has been overpraised by those who have reviewed this film. His sets and props look like papier mache objects which have been painted by three-year-olds. Adding to the bizarre feeling of the enterprise are the life-size puppets themselves, who never seem real, but remind one of those men and women who parade around theme parks in such getups, fooling no one but the smallest tots.

This film has received little if any notice over the years, and is only occasionally revived on television. Unfortunately as the eighties draw to a close the Kroffts have once again found some measure of fame as the creators of those ever-present celebrity-look-alike puppets. But even if they themselves continue to survive in an industry devoted more and more to juvenalia, at least there is one consolation to those with taste and intelligence: the fruits of their labors have always been and will forever continue to be considered junk.

Willy Wonka and the Chocolate Factory

A David L. Wolper Production, *released by* Paramount Pictures, 1971. *Producers* David L. Wolper and Stan Margulies. *Director* Mel Stuart. *Screenplay* Roald Dahl, *based on his book Charlie and the Chocolate Factory. Additional Dialogue (uncredited)* David Seltzer. *Director of Photography* Arthur Ibbetson, B.S.C. *Musical Supervision and Scoring* Walter Scharf. *Editor* David Saxon. *Art Director* Harper Goff. *Special Effects* Logan R. Frazee. *Sound* Karsten Ullrich. *Sound Editor* Charles L. Campbell. *Music Editor* Jack Tillar. *Dialogue Coach* Frawley Becker. *Wardrobe* Ille Sievers. *Costume Designer* Helen Colvig. *Unit Manager* Renate Neuchl. *Construction Manager* Hendrik G. Wynands. *Associate Editor* Mel Shapiro. *Dance Arrangements* Betty Walberg. *Camera Operator* Paul Wilson. *Re-recording* Dick Portman. *Script Supervisor* Trudi Von Trotha. *Makeup* Raimund Stangl. *Hairstyles* Susi Krause. *Production Manager* Pia Arnold. *Choreography* Howard Jeffrey. *Assistant Directors* Jack Roe, Wolfgang Glattes. *Casting* Marion Dougherty Associates, Selway-Baker Ltd. Filmed at Bavaria Studios in Munich, Germany. Technicolor. Running time: 100 minutes.

Cast: Gene Wilder (Willy Wonka), Jack Albertson (Grandpa Joe), Peter Ostrum (Charlie Bucket), Michael Bollner (Augustus Gloop), Ursula Reit (Mrs. Gloop), Denise Nickerson (Violet Beauregarde), Leonard Stone (Mr. Beauregarde), Julie Dawn Cole (Veruca Salt), Roy Kinnear (Mr. Salt), Paris Themmen (Mike Teevee), Dodo Denny (Mrs. Teevee), Diana Sowle (Mrs. Bucket), Aubrey Woods (Mr. Bill), David Battley (Mr. Turkentine), Gunter Meissner (Mr. Slugworth), Peter Capell (Tinker), Werner J. Heyking (Jopeck), Ernst Ziegler (Grandpa George), Dora Altmann (Grandma Georgina), Franziska Liebing (Grandma Josephine).

Songs "The Candy Man," "Cheer Up, Charlie," "(I've Got a) Golden Ticket," "Pure Imagination," "Oompa-Loompa-Doompadee-Doo," "I Want it Now" music by Anthony Newley, lyrics by Leslie Bricusse.

Willy Wonka and the Chocolate Factory, perhaps the most

oft-revived (and best) children's musical-fantasy picture after *Oz,* oddly enough came about *because of* a child's wish. Director Mel Stuart explains:

> The genesis for the movie *Willy Wonka and the Chocolate Factory* came from my daughter, who was four years old at the time. She had read the book by Roald Dahl *(Charlie and the Chocolate Factory)* and she loved it, and I was the vice-president of David Wolper Productions at the time and had directed several documentaries [like *The Making of the President*] and features [like *If It's Tuesday This Must be Belgium,* 1969], and I read the book, saw the possibilities for its turning into a very good screenplay, and brought the idea to Dave. At first we toyed with the idea of making an animated film, but then we decided to go ahead and make it a regular feature. Then Dave found out we could get Quaker Oats to put up the money, Quaker Oats went to Paramount to distribute it, and we were on the way. We had several major problems at the outset. First was "Do we put music in?" We finally decided that for this particular fantasy music would not be out of order. The second was finding Willy Wonka. We searched and searched, and finally arrived in New York and spoke to Joel Grey. Then one day we were at the Plaza Hotel and Gene Wilder walked in, and the minute he walked into the room — he had done *Stop the Revolution* and so forth but wasn't terribly widely known by that time, even though he had appeared in *The Producers* and *Bonnie and Clyde* also — I knew we had found our man. I remember running down the hall after him and stopping him at the elevator and saying to him: "You are going to do this picture, no two ways about it. You *are* Willy Wonka." The other problem was the music. Dave happened to be good friends with Anthony Newley and Leslie Bricusse, and I had heard their music and thought they'd be sensational for the picture.

But a still bigger problem came with the adaptation of Dahl's book. Mel Stuart says that "while the creation was all Roald Dahl's, his script didn't transfer so well to the screen, so we brought in a very gifted young man named David Seltzer [writer-director of the superb 1986 teen drama *Lucas*] who eventually did a good deal of rewriting." Seltzer, then 30, recalls that the experience was "my baptism by fire" into the film-writing business:

The wondrous Fizzy Lifting Drink.

"I had unsuccessfully been trying to convince people in the Hollywood community that I was worth being paid for screenwriting, and they took me up on it because they had an emergency . . . the script was a mess."

Dahl had written exactly what one would have expected, a direct transfer of his book to the screen, with all the characters and most of the dialogue intact. However, Stuart felt that the first 40 minutes or so (before the Willy Wonka character is introduced) needed more of a sharp, contemporary comic edge than that which was present in Dahl, so he asked Seltzer and a few other outsiders, including Bob Kaufman *(Love at First Bite)* to write a bunch of comedy skits involving people searching for Wonka Bars around the world—without consulting Dahl. However, the basic plotline of Dahl's story was retained (with other changes to be noted).

The film opens as it is announced to the world that Mr. Willy

Wonka, the world's most famous confectioner, has planted golden tickets inside five Wonka bars which entitle the lucky holders to a personal tour of his mystery-shrouded candy factory and a lifetime supply of chocolate. In the town where Wonka's factory is located, Charlie Bucket (Peter Ostrum) lives with his impoverished mother and four feeble grandparents. He dreams of becoming one of the winners.

Soon, the first four tickets are discovered. The winners are Augustus Gloop, a corpulent and gluttonous German boy; Violet Beauregarde, a gum-chewing brat and daughter of an American used car salesman; Veruca Salt, the spoiled daughter of a British peanut tycoon; and Mike Teevee, a surly lad who spends his life glued to his television set.

Charlie's faint hopes are shattered when news comes from South America that a shady millionaire type has found the last golden ticket. One day on the way home from school, he finds a silver coin in a raingutter, buys a Wonka bar for his Grandpa Joe, and then reads in a newspaper that the fifth ticket was a fraud. Tearing open the Wonka bar, Charlie discovers the last golden ticket. He then encounters an evil-looking man who says he is Oscar Slugworth, Willy Wonka's chief competitor. The man offers Charlie a bribe (he has done the same with the other winners) to steal one of Wonka's Everlasting Gobstoppers (a new kind of candy that never gets smaller) during his tour of the factory.

The kids are allowed to bring one member of their family to the factory. Charlie chooses Grandpa Joe (Jack Albertson), who leaves his bed for the first time in 20 years. Assembling at the candy factory at the designated time, the five children are greeted by the enigmatic Willy Wonka (Gene Wilder), a foppishly attired man with a sardonic sense of humor who warns them to follow his instructions (he even insists that all the children sign a standard form of contract before proceeding).

Wonka shows a dazzling array of wonders to his guests: the Chocolate Room, where everything is edible; the S.S. Wonkatania, which travels on a river of chocolate; lickable flavored wallpaper; the Inventing room, where each child receives his prized Everlasting Gobstopper; and the Oompa-Loompas (green-haired midgets that run the factory).

One by one the children disobey Wonka's orders, are severely punished, and disqualified. Only Charlie remains. But to his and Grandpa Joe's surprise, when they ask about the lifetime supply of chocolate (Wonka has dismissed them without mention of it), Wonka angrily orders them out of the factory for trying the Fizzy-Lifting Drink and bouncing off Wonka's spotless ceiling. He claims the contract is null and void. Grandpa Joe is furious and suggests to Charlie that they give Slugworth the gobstopper sample. But honest Charlie takes the candy from his pocket and hands it over to Wonka. A smile spreads over Wonka's face. He has found the one good child he has been searching for. Slugworth appears. He is actually a Wonka secret agent hired to test the children's honesty. Only Charlie passed.

Willy takes Charlie and Grandpa Joe for a flight in his Great Glass Wonkavator. As they sail over the city, Willy tells Charlie that he has chosen him as his heir and that he and his family are to move into the factory, where Charlie will succeed Willy as the world's most famous chocolate maker.

The final script is just as reflective of Seltzer's personality as Dahl's—perhaps even more so. Certainly Seltzer made some important improvements on Dahl's original conception. Chief among them was the decision to eliminate the character of Charlie's father, who in the book was a worker in a toothpaste factory. He had no real significance in terms of the protagonist, Charlie (the book, recall, was called *Charlie and the Chocolate Factory*), with whom he had no contact whatsoever. What Seltzer has done is to shift the focus of Charlie's world to two things—his family (his four bedridden grandparents), whom he helps support through his daily paper route (his mother is a widow and works herself at a laundry)—in particular his Grandpa Joe, to whom he feels closest (and when he is given the opportunity to bring one family member to the factory, it is he whom Charlie chooses)—and his obsessive quest to find a golden ticket (toward which goal Grandpa Joe encourages him by giving up tobacco in order to spend his money on Wonka Bars).

But there is a hint that despite Charlie's attachment to Grandpa Joe, there is an important element missing from his life

Wonka orders Grandpa Joe and Charlie out of the factory for trying Fizzy Lifting Drink without permission. Stuart: "I don't know what kids make of this scene."

(as one of his grandparents acknowledges), and thus, as Henry Blinder observes in his essay on the film in *Cult Movies,* "The story becomes a boy's search for his father's—surrogate Willy Wonka's—approval (and the title of the film was changed to *Willy Wonka and the Chocolate Factory*). Throughout the film, we and Charlie are constantly trying to break through the barrier that separates a boy from the most important man in his life."

Connected with this theme is another, still more clever Seltzer touch—the invention of the Slugworth character and the Everlasting Gobstopper "test." It adds an extra element of suspense of Dahl's one-by-one elimination of the bad children through punishment (and we get hints throughout—though only from Slugworth—that Slugworth and Wonka are favoring Charlie to win), culminating with the final scene, in which only

Charlie remains and, unbeknownst to him, must pass one final obstacle—handing the candy back to Wonka after the latter viciously dismisses him and, as Grandpa Joe puts it, "smashes all his dreams to pieces." "I really don't know what kids make of this scene (which is shocking, to say the least—Wonka has acted coldly throughout, but never to this extreme) the first time they see the picture," says director Stuart (though he observes that "if you watch the picture closely you'll notice that Gene's hair becomes more and more unwieldy as the story progresses, so by the time the climactic scene in the office comes up, you'll be able to see that he really is quite mad"). Fortunately, because of Seltzer's considerable skill in balancing sweetness and terror, if you will, it emerges, as Blinder says, as "the supreme moment in the film (as) the parental veil of mystery (drops), transforming Wonka into a warm human being."

Even more glorious is the final scene in the Wonkavator in which Wonka reveals to Charlie that he is giving the factory to him. Like the ending of Seltzer's *Lucas,* this is a moment of perfect vindication—in this case for the Wonka character—and a wonderful surprise which works beautifully without a single excess drop of sentiment. Incidentally, as Stuart and Seltzer tell it, there is a funny story behind the search for the last line of the picture (as Wonka, holding Charlie back after giving him the news, reminds him, seemingly to temper his excitement, "But don't forget what happened to the man who suddenly got everything he always wanted." When Charlie asks what happened, Wonka surprisingly replies, "He lived happily ever after").

Stuart:

> We didn't have a closing line yet when we went to shoot the scene—everybody had for some reason forgotten about it. So I was desperate for an ending, and I got on the phone to Seltzer, who had returned to the U.S.A. (the picture was shot at Bavaria Studios in Munich, Germany) and was vacationing in the Maine woods! We finally tracked him down after a long wait—I had a telephone line open from *Munich* to *Maine* for something like an *hour*—and after I explained the situation to him, he went off by himself for five minutes and came back with the wonderful line that now ends the picture.

Concerning the line itself, Seltzer adds this: "I racked my brain for that fateful last line. I knew it had to be great, so I researched the greatest last lines of all time. And I used one. Albeit with a slight twist (namely, the 'set-up'), I knew that any story that ended with the words 'He lived happily ever after' couldn't be all bad."

Seltzer's ability to create gentle, touching scenes which deftly avoid sticky-sweetness is evident throughout the first section of the picture in the dialogues delineating the relations between Charlie and his impoverished family, which could easily have become uncomfortable, particularly as Charlie is depicted as so unusually good-natured and nice (though, as Blinder observes, he is not a hero, just a boy, not without thoughts of his own happiness). There are numerous heartwarming moments, such as Charlie's arriving home breathless with the ticket, astonishing everyone, and after reading it, telling Grandpa Joe, "I wish you could go with me," to which the old man—who has been bedridden for 20 years—responds by climbing—with assistance—out of bed without a second thought.

The key here, of course, is simplicity and honesty. Another earlier scene in which Charlie comes to the laundry to visit his mother and tell her he's given up searching for Golden Tickets stands out also:

> CHARLIE: They found the third ticket today.
> MOTHER: Did they?
> CHARLIE: Yeah. That means there're only two tickets left. Just two. Pretty soon, just one.
> MOTHER: Well, I wonder who the lucky ones will be.
> CHARLIE: Well, just in case you're wondering if it'll be me, it won't be. Just in case you're interested you can count me out.
> MOTHER: Charlie. There are 100 billion people in this world, and only five of them will find golden tickets. Even if you had a sackful of money you probably wouldn't find one, and after this contest is over you'll be no different from the billions of others who didn't find one.
> CHARLIE: But I *am* different. I want it more than any of them.
> MOTHER: Charlie, you'll get your chance. One day things will change.
> CHARLIE: When? When will they change?
> MOTHER: Probably when you least expect it. See you later.

This brings up another intriguing element which Seltzer added to the scenario, the surprise uncovering of the emergence of a phony golden ticket (whose perpetrator was nicely delineated as an anonymous selfish sleazeball from a foreign country — a multimillionaire who needed a lifetime supply of chocolate about as much as he needed another gambling casino; he makes a nice contrast to the poor Grandpa Joe and company who watch the announcement of his "find" on TV — in their pathetic little hovel, they cannot begin to comprehend such an injustice). In Dahl's book, Charlie simply found the missing fifth ticket one day.

This preoccupation with creating suspense through unexpected revelations adds considerably to the emotional impact of the basic theme of the tale — namely, that fundamental honesty and selflessness are all that matters, and that if one keeps these elements inside him and resists all temptation, he will be rewarded with the moon (or, in this case, a chocolate factory — a good enough substitute for a small boy) — *Wonka* is practically the only film after *Oz* to offer such an obvious moral concern. We see throughout the hour-long episode in the factory that Charlie (and Grandpa Joe) are the only ones who are really enjoying themselves, since they are not preoccupied with plotting to screw Wonka behind his back. Also, Charlie is the only one who is not just looking out for himself — when Augustus Gloop, the fat kid, falls into the chocolate factory, only Charlie tries to help him, and at the end, when it turns out he is the only one left, the first words out of his mouth are not "When do I get my candy?" but rather "What's going to happen to the other kids?"

This brings up the issue toward which most of the film's criticism has been leveled — the harsh treatment of the children who disobey Wonka's orders while in the factory. Director Stuart (who in person exudes the same nutty sensibility which characterizes the film and who had much to do with shaping the film's feel and outlook) has a succinct and perfectly logical explanation for their existence (they were present in the book also): "I wasn't doing a Disney piece. The kids *had* to be punished if they were bad." One must also remember that the effects — though seemingly hideous at the time — are only temporary:

Wonka tells Charlie at the end that all of the bad children will, before leaving, be "completely restored to their normal, terrible selves—though perhaps they'll be a bit wiser for the ware." (Also, this angle is what lends true contemporaneity to the film and helps to give it more appeal than other goody-goodyish kids' fantasies—for as Roger Ebert remarks, "Kids are not sugar and spice, not very often, and they appreciate the poetic justice when a bad kid gets what's coming to him.") Stuart reminds viewers that he "never thought of *Wonka* as a children's film. I treated all the child actors like adults, because I always felt this was an adult's picture primarily. There were a lot of quotes from Shakespeare in the course of the film which were deliberately put there by me." Among them is Wonka's scolding of the disbelieving Veruca Salt ("Whoever heard of a snozberry?" she asks after he describes one of the flavors of his lickable wallpaper) with "We are the music-makers, and we are the dreamers of the dreams."

Most of these other references also serve to break the barrier between audience/spectator in the factory and Wonka's world and allow them to accept anything that appears. One delicious bit is Wonka's initial explanation of the origins of the Oompa-Loompas to the parents and children: "They came from Loompaland," to which one of the mothers replies, "Mr. Wonka, I am a teacher of geography, and there is no such place"—to which Wonka counters with, "Well, then, if you teach geography, you know all about it, and what a terrible place it is, full of wangdoodles and hornswagglers and horrible vermicious knits..."

Most of Stuart's other attempts at adult humor are present in the comedy skits in the first 40 minutes of the film concerning the mad search for Wonka Bars. One bit that was eliminated unfortunately came a little *too close* to everyday reality. Stuart explains:

> The skit went like this: a man goes to the top of a mountain where a guru sits and says, "I'm an explorer. I spent five years trying to reach the top of this mountain, and in the process I've lost all the members of my party. All I want to know, Great Guru, is what is the secret of life?" The Guru asks, "You got Wonka Bar?" The man gives him the bar and asks his

Director Mel Stuart (directly behind camera) checks angle for shot of Golden Ticket.

question again. The Guru opens up the Wonka Bar hoping to find a Golden Ticket, and there's no ticket inside, so he throws the Wonka Bar to the ground and he looks at the man and says: "Life is a disappointment." Now, I thought this was really funny, and we'd shot the scene exactly as I described it — must have spent $25,000 on that scene alone — but at the previews, nobody laughed! So I took a psychiatrist to a private screening with me and I asked him to explain to me why nobody though the gag was funny, and he looked at me, and he said, "Mel, it's because for most people in the theater, life *is* a disappointment." So we threw that out.

Most of the ones that remain are quite good, however: in one, a woman whose husband is being held for ransom is telephoned by the kidnappers and told that they will give him back if she surrenders her case of Wonka Bars. She hesitates, asking a detective: "How long will they give me to think it over?" Another has an auction culminating with the highest bid from an offscreen *Queen Elizabeth* (neatly recalled at the end when Wonka tells Charlie and Grandpa Joe that he "must answer that note from the Queen" — who of course is angered that she didn't find a ticket).

Here are a couple of interesting sidelights on this angle from Stuart:

> There was a bit of a flak at the time — 1970 — a lot of people in the black community resented the fact that the book was called "Charlie and the *Chocolate* Factory," and they felt there was a hidden meaning because the "oompa-loompa" characters were brown. *I* felt I didn't want them to be natives from Africa anyway. I felt that they should be strange, though, so I went ahead and had the green wigs and orange faces applied . . . also, a lot of people over the years have said they thought I was doing a psychedelic LSD number with the mushrooms in the factory. You know, because after they taste them they go down into the river in the boat where everything gets crazy.

Despite the fact that Stuart is not always terribly adroit with a camera — like many of the directors of these films, he is a veteran of TV, though superior to any one of the others mentioned thus far (though one number, "The Candy Man," does come off like a commercial for Wonka candy) — much of the appeal of the film in general and of the fantasy sequences in particular derives from his direction. One notable pre-factory touch is Charlie's discovery of the ticket: Stuart creates a wonderful sense of excitement and anticipation around the moment before Charlie opens the Wonka Bar to disclose the Golden Ticket by having the voices of the local citizens expressing their consternation over the fraud involving the fifth ticket heard faintly but distinctly enough in the background as Charlie walks away from them toward camera and then takes out the bar. The same sort of feeling pervades the scene where all the people gathered at the factory await the arrival of ten o'clock and Willy Wonka's entrance. When he does appear, he is walking with a cane—Stuart cuts to a reaction shot of Charlie, who is worried about his health—but at the last minute relinquishes it and does a surprise somersault, landing on his feet (Stuart says this was Gene Wilder's idea, and that he worked for weeks with a troupe of acrobats to perfect it). And there is the entrance into the factory and the pan across the wondrous chocolate room which recalls Dorothy's first view of Munchkinland in *Oz*—culminating in Wonka's bowing to the spectators and allowing them to explore freely its contents.

With regard to the various gimmicks in the factory themselves, Stuart says, "I tried to maintain the highest amount of reality as I could. The only way to make fantasy believable is to make it as real as possible." Not many people who see the film know this, but every single thing in the factory—with the exception of the chocolate river—was *really edible*, exactly what is was supposed to be in the film! That includes the lickable wallpaper too. Many people have complained that Harper Goff's sets—particularly the Chocolate Room and the river ("something I'd fantastized about since I was a boy," says Stuart), which to some threatens to look like waste products—are a big letdown, never seeming real enough. Now that this heretofore undisclosed (Stuart had never before been interviewed about the film) information about the wonders therein have been revealed, perhaps they will think twice about their initial judgments (and the river is thick and bubbly enough that it too seems edible).

Besides the candy, other effects are impressive also, for instance the bubble machine which whisks Charlie and Grandpa Joe up to the roof of the factory. Stuart says that this was no trick: the actors were really up there on strings, very high, and it was quite dangerous. Another excellently executed sequence is the Satanic boat ride—to many the film's high point—mainly due to the seamlessly integrated process shots. A few of the effects—such as the shrunken Mike Teevee and the Wonkamobile which is "squeezedried"—don't come off nearly as well, but they are in the minority. One nice odd touch is the decor in Wonka's office—everything is cut in half, in keeping with his off-center, backward logic ("We have so much time and so little to do," he often says, then asks everyone to "strike that, reverse it"; other gems are "If the good Lord had intended us to walk, he wouldn't have invented roller skates," and "And so shines a good deed in a weary world," after Charlie hands over the gobstopper).

But perhaps the film's biggest virtue is the casting of Gene Wilder as Wonka ("a very risky venture," says Stuart, "because, remember, our star doesn't come on until 40 minutes into the picture—and even then, Wilder wasn't a big name yet"). This may come as a great shock to many who have seen the film over and over and have grown accustomed to Wilder, but according to Leslie Bricusse, who wrote the lyrics for the film's songs, *Fred Astaire* (who was a friend of Bricusse's and told him this) wanted the part when the project was first announced, but apparently he never informed producer David Wolper about it. It's just as well: with all due respect to the great man, at 72 he was simply too old (as he had proven three years earlier in the disastrous musical *Finian's Rainbow*) for the demands of such a part. But even if Astaire could have managed it, he would not have been able to imbue the character with the maniacal edge which makes Wilder's Wonka stand out in the memory. Wilder had the following to say about the part in an early seventies interview:

> We all grew up on movies with scenes where the actor is lying, and you know he's lying, but he wants to make *sure* you know it's a lie, and so he overacts and all but winks at you, and everybody in the world except for the girl he's talking to knows he's lying. I want to do the opposite. To *really* lie, and fool the audience.... I wanted people to wonder if Willy Wonka was telling the truth so that you wouldn't really know until the end of the picture what Willy's motivations were.

As I have made clear, Wilder certainly has all the best lines in the picture, and makes the most of them at every opportunity. He is certainly more sinister and enigmatic than Dahl's Wonka, but also, paradoxically, more endearing (and the role is his most memorable to date), because he makes the sudden transition to benevolent father-figure just as believable as his earlier self by imbuing it with the same unflagging intensity. Joel Grey (the original choice), might conceivably have come close, but as Blinder says, "it is inconceivable to imagine anyone else in the role." (Grey was to perfect a similar role the following year in *Cabaret*—which, coincidentally, was shot on the very same soundstage as *Wonka*— and Bob Fosse even employed some of the same technical personnel, such as assistant director Wolfgang Glattes, who came to be one of his regulars.)

Peter Ostrum's Charlie is something of a problem. He seems unsure of himself in the early scenes of the film, and doesn't seem to have a really strong grip on the role ("I was basically playing myself," says Ostrum, 28 years old and a veterinarian in 1989—he gave up acting after this film, feeling he'd never have another part as special), occasionally veering toward the saccharine. This might have been helped if Stuart had restrained him a bit, but Ostrum somehow still earns the audience's sympathy.

The late Jack Albertson, a character actor who made far too few appearances in film—he is best remembered for his role in *The Subject Was Roses* (1968), for which he received an Oscar, and his bit part as a mail clerk in 1947's *Miracle on 34th Street*—is a perfect Grandpa Joe. His leaping about the dingy Bucket shack singing "I've Got a Golden Ticket" is a riotous moment, and he also is spunky and sharp, with some good wisecracks at the other indulgent parents (though finally he too evidences a greedy side when he suggests to Charlie that they sell the Gobstopper to Slugworth after Wonka tells them off). All of the children are just right also (Stuart and Howard Jeffrey, who choreographed the numbers, particularly recall Julie Dawn Cole, who played spoiled Veruca Salt, as a most promising young talent—though one which apparently never blossomed), though their parts are relatively minor, as are those of the other adults, including veteran character actor Roy Kinnear.

What then are *Wonka*'s shortcomings? It does have some notable ones. The most obvious is that the film is terribly uneven in terms of style (as Pauline Kael said, "It's stilted and frenetic, like Prussians at play"). The opening 40 minutes consisting of the comedy skits intercut with scenes depicting Charlie's home life contrasts harshly with the remaining hour, all of which is spent in the fantastic factory. Much of this has to do with the rather

"The Candy Man": Aubrey Woods.

meager budget on the picture (most of the money obviously went to the creation of the factory sets) — though the filmmakers partly get away with this because Charlie is supposed to live in a poor neighborhood. The whereabouts for the factory is not specified, but one assumes that it's in the United States, so the fact that the locations were shot in Munich definitely creates something of a disorienting feeling.

Adding to this impression is the fact that almost all of the songs in the film are heard during the opening section. Bricusse says he does not understand at all why the producers only wanted half a score. As it is, he describes the numbers as "puerile," and he is pretty much correct. "Tony Newley and I thought 'Pure Imagination' was going to be the showstopper, but it was horrendously mutilated by the way they choreographed it. Gene Wilder walks into the factory, sings two bars, then takes an interminable pause, then sings another two, then another pause." Also, Bricusse says he abhors the fact that they used the "Oompa loompa" chants so many times (they take the place of the lack of songs in the second half), calling them an "embarrassment." He is right here also — though many of Walter Scharf's arrangements in the dramatic sections of the picture are good (and he composed a beautiful overture). Stuart says he sometimes removes "Cheer Up Charlie" from TV prints because it tends to slow the picture down.

With regard to the now-legendary "Candy Man" ("the only good song in the picture besides 'Pure Imagination,'" says Bricusse), Bricusse (and Stuart) deeply regret the fact that it was performed by a non-singer (actor Aubrey Woods). Stuart says, however, that originally the part of Bill, the candy man, was conceived as being either Anthony Newley or Sammy Davis, Jr., but "I didn't want anyone for the part who was too well known, since that would distract the audience and take the picture out of the realm of fantasy." That the song became the megahit that it did was a very unlikely thing, considering that it came from a children's film which appeared only briefly during the summer months before vanishing from sight. Actually, Sammy Davis is rumored to have hated it upon first hearing it, but eventually decided that since it was written by Bricusse and Newley, who had given him other successes such as "What Kind of Fool Am I?" it was worth giving it a try. The rest is history, but unfortunately Davis' hit came in 1972, a year after the film was released, so Bricusse and Newley missed out on a "Best Song" Oscar nomination — a pity, since, as Bricusse points out, the song that won for 1971 wasn't even technically a song — the theme from *Shaft*!

But despite these flaws — and the fact that the film received almost no attention on initial release (Stuart says, "I think the reason had a lot to do with the fact that the country was in unrest and there was a lot of cynicism because of the war in Vietnam, the civil rights movement, etc. I think if it had opened in the '80s it would have done a lot better"), *Willy Wonka* has endured, becoming, as Stuart points out, probably the best children's musical-fantasy picture after *Oz*, thanks to frequent revivals on TV and at colleges (and now it is finally available on videocassette). He does not know whether Roald Dahl liked the result (he probably resented the unauthorized changes in his text, though in deference to him he was given sole screen credit), but regardless, *Willy Wonka* will continue to endure for generations to come.

Bedknobs and Broomsticks

A Walt Disney Pictures Production, *released by* Buena Vista, 1971. *Producer* Bill Walsh. *Director* Robert Stevenson. *Screenplay* Bill Walsh and Don DaGradi, *from the book by* Mary Norton. *Director of Photography* Frank Phillips, A.S.C. *Art Directors* John B. Mansbridge, Peter Ellenshaw. *Music composed, arranged and conducted by* Irwin Kostal. *Choreography* Donald McKayle. *Editor* Cotton Warburton. *Set Decorators* Emile Kuri, Hal Gausman. *Costumes* Bill Thomas, Chuck Keehne, Emily Sundby. *Assistant to Designer* Shelby Anderson. *Titles* David Jones. *Dance Accompanist* Albert Mellor. *Assistant Choreographer* Carolyn Dyer. *Second Unit Director* Arthur J. Vitarelli. *Technical Consultants* Manford Lating, Milt Larsen, James McInnes, Bob Baker, Spungbuggy Works. *Animation Director* Ward Kimball. *Animation* Milt Kahl, Art Stevens, John Lounsbery, Julius Svends, Eric Larson, Hal King, Fred Hellmich, Jack Buckley, Jack Boyd. *Sound Supervisor* Robert O. Cook. *Sound Mixer* Dean Thomas. *Makeup* Robert J. Schiffer. *Hairstylist* La Rue Matheron. *Assistant Director* Christopher Hibler. *Script Supervisor* Lois Thurman. *Music Editor* Evelyn Kennedy. *Assistant to the Conductor* James MacDonald. *Animation Story* Ralph Wright, Ted Berman. *Layout* Don Griffith, Joe Hale. *Animation-Live-Action Design* McLaren Stewart. *Backgrounds* Al Dempster, Dick Kelsey, Bill Layne, Ralph Hulete. *Animation Film Editor* James W. Swain. *Special Effects* Alan Maley, Eustace Lycett, Danny Lee. Technicolor. Running time: 112 minutes.

Cast Angela Lansbury (Miss Price), David Tomlinson (Emilius), Roddy McDowell (Mr. Jelk), Sam Jaffe (Bookman), John Ericson (Col. Heiler), Bruce Forsyth (Swinburne), Cindy O'Callaghan (Carrie), Roy Snart (Paul), Ian Weighill (Charlie), Tessie O'Shea (Mrs. Hobday), Arthur E. Gould-Porter (Capt. Greer), Ben Wrigley (Portobello Road Workman), Reginald Owen (General Teagler), Cyril Delevanti (Elderly Farmer), Rick Traeger, Manfred Lating, John Orchard (German Sergeants), Robert Holt (Voice of Codfish), Lennie Weinrib (Voice of Secretary Bird & Lion), Dal McKennon (Voice of Bear).

Songs "The Old Home Guard," "The Age of Not Believing," "A Step in the Right Direction," "Eglantine/Don't Let Me Down," "Portobello Road," "The Beautiful Briny," "Substitutiary Locomotion," music and lyrics by Richard M. and Robert B. Sherman.

Bedknobs and Broomsticks was the Disney Studio's attempt to recapture the magic of *Mary Poppins*. It was the organization's most expensive and ambitious effort since *Poppins* and following the death of Walt in 1966. Reunited were producer Bill Walsh, scenarist Don DaGradi, Robert Stevenson, the Sherman Brothers, actor David Tomlinson, Irwin Kostal and the special effects team headed by Eustace Lycett. Like *Poppins,* the plot was a mixture of the real and the fantastic, set again in England, this time in the seaside village of Pepperinge Eye during World War II, centering around the activities of prim Eglantine Price (Angela Lansbury), whose life abruptly changes when she reluctantly takes in three young evacuees from London (Ian Weighill, Roy Snart, Cindy O'Callaghan). Miss Price is a determined young lady who is convinced that, through sorcery, she can aid the British war effort. Toward that end she is taking a correspondence course from the Emelius Browne College of Witchcraft.

When the children discover her secret, a bargain is made. In return for their silence, Eglantine gives them a magic bedknob that will, when placed in the post of an old brass bed, take them anywhere they wish. Free from interference, Eglantine eagerly awaits her final lesson in witchcraft . . . only to receive word that Professor Browne has closed his school for the duration.

With the help of the magic bedknob, Eglantine and the children set out for London in search of the Professor and the final spell. There they find him (David Tomlinson), only to discover that he is a humbug who is amazed to learn his witchcraft works. Hoping to entice Eglantine on the stage with her magic, Browne agrees to help her find the last lesson which is contained in a missing book.

Here begin the adventures of the unlikely quintet as they search for the mysterious spell. Their journey takes them to a meeting with the evil Bookman (Sam Jaffe), and to the storybook isle of Naboombu where Eglantine finds the talisman enabling her to practice "Substitutiary Locomotion," the animation of inanimate objects.

When a Nazi landing party invades Pepperinge Eye, Eglantine uses substitutiary locomotion to summon up a ghostly medieval army which repels the raiders before Miss Price loses her magical power — and her heart to Professor Browne.

Unfortunately, in the final analysis, all of this promising-sounding stuff adds up to very little, proving once again the truth behind the old dictums that lightning never strikes twice in the same place, and that money can't buy artistic success. The problems begin first with the scenario by Walsh and DaGradi. While the premise itself is intriguing, it is poorly realized. There is a startling lack of attention paid to logical detail in the exposition and character introductions (including that of Miss Price), and as a result, the film starts with a whimper instead of a bang and never really gains any significant momentum.

Also, director Stevenson was by now getting on in years (he was 65) and had lost his formerly sharp storytelling sense (his work on Disney's 1969 *The Love Bug* had been remarkable only in the action sequences — where, no doubt, he had been helped by a second unit). Scenes are staged limply and with little energy or flair: the film looks like the work of a very tired man. There is evidence of generous expenditure throughout, but neither the director nor the scenarists are able to create or sustain interest in the proceedings for very long.

Of course, the lack of a sense of believability is not helped either by embarrassingly poor special effects. The scene wherein the bed containing Miss Price and her charges takes off and heads for London was, of course, the filmmakers' big chance (and the picture's crucial moment), and they threw it completely out the door: even the most cinematically naive viewer can discern the obvious fakery of the sudden cut from the real bedroom (though the effect was supposed to be "disguised" by swirling colors) to a process shot (against a blue posterboard backdrop) of the bed "flying" across the skies that looks like it was pasted on (reprehensible indeed from the team that worked on *Poppins;* by comparison, the effects in *Chitty* and *Dolittle* almost seem

Publicity photo of Lansbury, Tomlinson and the children.

sophisticated! But this incompetence was yet to be topped six years later in another Disney production, *Pete's Dragon,* as we shall see). The scene that is often commented upon is the one wherein David Tomlinson engages in a basketball game with a team of animated animals on the isle of Naboombu. Suffice it to say that the result is not half as impressive as similar sequences in *Poppins, Song of the South* or any of a handful of other ventures — ditto the finale in which inanimate suits of armor are suddenly moved to action.

The choreography on the film (credited to Carolyn Dyer) is nil also (the potentially big moment here was the "Portobello Road" number, but the effect is scattershot at best): why couldn't Wood and Breaux have been recruited? They're not Hermes Pan, but they're not bad either. The Sherman Brothers' score, though, is pleasant and lively, with their usual clever ditties ("Substitutiary Locomotion" was intended to be *Bedknobs'*

The "Portobello Road" number.

"Supercalifragilisticexpialidocious"—it doesn't quite match it, though), but not as memorable as *Poppins*', though there is one excellent song, "The Age of Not Believing," sung by Lansbury, which was nominated for an Oscar. Unfortunately, the renditions (except perhaps for Tomlinson's "With a Flair," which inexplicably is missing from many prints) are lackluster, however.

Finally, a comment about the performers. Lansbury, a seasoned actress and an old pro, is always game, but was defeated by her material. Watching her teamed with Tomlinson, it is easy to see why he was given a *supporting* role in *Poppins;* there is no real chemistry between them, and the lack of a commanding presence at the center of all of this (as Julie Andrews' was) becomes felt early on (but also Lansbury's character is not nearly as interesting as Mary Poppins, a fault which can be attributed entirely to the writers). Also, the children, Ian Weighill and Cindy O'Callaghan, are dull, only pale imitations of Matthew

Garber and Karen Dotrice. Roddy McDowell and Sam Jaffe are totally wasted.

Although released at Christmastime, *Bedknobs* was not a smashing success with moviegoers, and proved to be the Disney Studio's last superproduction. Clearly the influence of Uncle Walt during his lifetime (despite the fact that his only credit on the features had been "Walt Disney Presents") had been more pervasive than anyone had imagined, as many undoubtedly realized after viewing this latest venture.

Alice's Adventures in Wonderland

A Josef Shaftel Production, *released by* American National, 1972, British. *Executive Producer* Josef Shaftel. *Associate Producer* Rene Dupont. *Producer* Derek Horne. *Director* William Sterling. *Screenplay* William Sterling, *from the novel by* Lewis Carroll. *Director of Photography* Geoffrey Unsworth, B.S.C. *Editor* Peter Weatherley. *Music* John Barry. *Lyrics* Don Black. *Choreography* Terry Gilbert. *Production Manager* Jack Causley. *Art Director* Norman Dorme. *Assistant Director* Bert Batt. *Camera Operator* Peter MacDonald. *Sound Editor* James Shields. *Music Editor* Michael Clifford. *Continuity* Maggie Unsworth. *Sound Recording* Bob Jones, Ken Ritchie. *Special Effects* Ted Samuels, Doug Ferris, Ron Whyerow. *Wardrobe Master* Ron Beck. *Wardrobe Mistress* Dorothy Edwards. *Hairdresser* Roddy Crystal. *Construction Manager* Dick Frift. *Assistant Editor* Peter Culverwell. *Makeup* Stuart Freeborn. *Costume Designer* Anthony Mendleson. *Production Designer* Michael Stringer. Todd-AO. Eastman Colour. Running time: 97 minutes.

Cast Fiona Fullerton (Alice), Michael Crawford (The White Rabbit), Robert Helpmann (The Mad Hatter), Peter Sellers (The March Hare), Dudley Moore (The Dormouse), Ralph Richardson (The Caterpillar), Peter Bull (The Duchess), Dame Flora Robson (The Queen of Hearts), Dennis Price (The King of Hearts), Spike Milligan (The Gryphon), Michael Hordern (The Mock Turtle), Freddie Cox (Tweedledum), Frank Cox (Tweedledee), Davy Kaye (Mouse), Hywel Bennett (Buckworth), Rodney Beves (Knave of Hearts), Ray Brooks (5 of Spades), Richard Warwick (7 of Spades), Dennis Waterman (2 of Spades), Julian Chagrin (Bill the Lizard), Patsy Rowlands (Cook), Freddy Earlle (Guinea Pig Pat), Michael Layston (Dogson), William Ellis (Dodo), Mike Elles (Guinea Pig 2), Peter O'Farrell (Fish Footman), Ian Trigger (Frog Footman), Victoria Shallard (Lorina), Pippa Vickers (Edith), Ray Edwards (Eagle), Stanley Bates (Monkey), Melita Manger (Squirrel), Angela Morgan (Lory), June Kidd (Magpie), Michael Reardon (Frog), Brian Tipping (Duck).

Music and Lyrics by John Barry and Don Black: "Curioser and Curioser," "Last World is Mine," "You've Gotta Know When to Stop," "Royal Procession," "Dum & Dee Dance & Nursery Rhyme," "Pun Song," "I've Never Been This Far Before," "Me I Never Knew," "Lobster Quadrille," "Will You Walk a Little Faster," "They Told Me You Had Been to Her."

How appropriate it was that in 1972, the 100th anniversary of the publication of Lewis Carroll's *Through the Looking Glass*, a new film based on that story should have been released. Also exciting was the announcement that it would be the first non–Americanized version of the tale (a criticism which had plagued the 1951 Walt Disney animated feature), and the only one to attempt to find live-action equivalents for the Tenniel drawings in the original. A wonderfully ambitious concept, to be sure, but there was one slight problem: the film which resulted was a total dud from start to finish.

Again, the chief culprit responsible for the disaster, the director (or in this case writer-director), was a man versed exclusively in television—one William Sterling, a Britisher who during production stated that he had been "living with the idea of filming *Alice* since 1965" because "no one has yet caught the true spirit of Lewis Carroll on the screen. What attracted me about the book was the incredible Victorian stillness within the closed world, opening out into realms of pure imagination. These are stories which only the modern widescreen cinema can get anywhere near." (*London Times,* July 30, 1972, p. 34.)

In terms of adaptation, Sterling's script was indeed more faithful to the original story than Disney and his team had been. One aspect that Sterling retained was the book's opening, a rendering of the "golden afternoon" of July 4, 1862, when Carroll (Dodgson in the story) and his companion Duckworth boated down the Isis with the three Liddell children and stopped to lounge on a mossy bank, where the children encouraged Dodgson to relate the story of Alice. The Disney film began with a fabricated opening with Alice's older sister reading to her on the bank, after which Alice grew bored and, spotting a white rabbit, chased after him.

Unfortunately, touches like this added up to very little, since

Top: *Alice (Fiona Fullerton) talks to Caterpillar (Ralph Richardson).*
Bottom: *Alice and the Queen of Hearts (Flora Robson).*

in transferring Carroll's images to the live-action format, Sterling merely succeeded in making everything seem heavy-handed. The Disney cartoon has been accused of lacking warmth, but at least in general it was lively and genuinely wondrous. Sterling's film is flat and tedious from the first minutes, and never recovers, though with the episodic nature of the story, one keeps hoping that eventually it will perk up.

The reason the film plods along like deadwood is due to Sterling's inability to manipulate the actors amid the meticulous settings in a way which would make everything seem real and interesting (he ignored Mel Stuart's credo that in order to make a fantasy believable, there must first be a basis in reality). Not surprisingly, the result seemed to be the inevitable outcome of his professed approach: "What attracted me about the book was the incredible Victorian stillness within the closed world." Stillness is what he got, all right: the film is a good cure for insomnia.

Also not helping were the costumes which in most cases completely smothered the actors' features, prohibiting any human feeling from surfacing (this had been one of the hallmarks of the costumes in *Oz*). Consequently, the actors' prancing about made them look positively ludicrous — not helped by the unspeakable choreography (originally, Robert Helpmann had wanted to handle it, but finally decided not to for fear that the ballet side would seem too important — what a pity).

But aside from the getups, particularly shameful is that Sterling had at his disposal a virtual grab bag of some of the greatest talents of the English stage and screen, names like Sir Ralph Richardson, Sir Robert Helpmann (making his second appearance in a children's film), Peter Sellers, Dudley Moore, Michael Crawford and Dame Flora Robson, and he was able to do nothing with them (though Robert Helpmann was able to sustain his Mad Hatter nicely) — perhaps he reasoned that these people wouldn't *need* much direction, but that notion was utter nonsense, as the film bears out. By contrast, Victor Fleming on *Oz*, working with good, not great — with the exception of Judy Garland — actors such as Ray Bolger, Jack Haley and Bert Lahr — was able to extract wondrous work from all concerned, which was no doubt a harder task than that which lay before Sterling.

In terms of song, this feature undoubtedly marks the low-point of the films explored in this book—as written by Don Murray and Don Black, they can barely be classified as such. There is not even a rhyme scheme in most cases, just a lot of arbitrary off-the-cuff verses that could have been written by nursery school children (remember the wonderful ditties in the Disney version like "Very Merry Unbirthday," "'Twas Brillig," and the ever-popular "I'm Late?"). In fact, they would comprise the most likely audience for this thoroughly tedious affair.

The Little Prince

A Paramount release, 1974. *Producer* Stanley Donen. *Associate Producer* A. Joseph Tandet. *Director* Stanley Donen. *Screenplay* Alan Jay Lerner, *based on the novel by* Antoine de Saint-Exupery. *Director of Photography* Christopher Challis, B.S.C. *Special Effects* Thomas Howard, F.R.P.S. and John Richardson. *Editors* Peter Boita, John Guthridge. *Art Director* Norman Reynolds. *Production Designer* John Barry. *Costumes* Shirley Russell, Tim Goodchild. *Choreographers* Bob Fosse ("Snake in the Grass"), Ronn Forella. *Musical Director* Douglas Gamley. *Orchestrations* Angela Morley. *Camera Operators* Freddie Cooper, John Palmer. *2nd Unit Photography* Paul Wilson. *Stills Cameraman* Keith Hamshere. *Sound Mixers* Jim Willis, John Richards, Bill Rowe. *Construction Managers* W.E. Welch, Jock Lyall. *Wardrobe Master* Charles Gu. *Makeup* Ernest Gass. *Hairdressers* Eileen Warren, Ronnie Cogg. *Unit Publicists* Gordon Arnold, John Richards. *Dubbing Editor* Jim Groom. *Special Effects Editor* Vernon Messenger. *Music Editor* Thelma Orr. *Production Manager* Al Burgess. *Assistant Directors* Allan James, Al Burgess. *Continuity* Pamela Carlton, Kay Mander, Marjorie Lavelly. *Production Executive* Arthur Carroll. *Production Manager* Eric Rattray. *Titles Designer* Maurice Binder. Technicolor. Running time: 88 minutes.

Cast Richard Kiley (The Pilot), Steven Warner (The Little Prince), Bob Fosse (The Snake), Gene Wilder (The Fox), Joss Ackland (The King), Clive Revill (The Businessman), Victor Spinetti (The Historian), Graham Crowden (The General), Donna McKechnie (The Rose).

Music and Lyrics by Frederick Loewe and Alan Jay Lerner: "It's a Hat/I Need Air," "Little Prince," "You're a Child," "Why Is the Desert?," "I'm on Your Side," "I Never Met a Rose," "Be Happy," "Closer and Closer and Closer," "Snake in the Grass."

According to author Joseph Casper, the film version of Antoine de Saint-Exupery's *The Little Prince* came about in the following manner:

[Although] from the beginning [Saint-Exupery's] slim volume of whimsey [had] tantalized filmmakers from Walt Disney to Orson Welles . . . it wasn't until the late sixties — when fantasy became, once again, a necessary antidote to the turmoil of the times — that serious work was begun on a film version of *The Little Prince.* . . .

A. Joseph Tandet, a theatrical lawyer and sometime producer, who had represented a playwright who had at one time optioned the property, shelled out six figures for the rights owned by Saint-Exupery's widow and Paris publisher Gallimard. Because the work was envisioned as a musical film, Alan J. Lerner was approached. An old friend of Tandet's and the celebrated librettist and lyricist of such Broadway hits as *Brigadoon* (1947), *Paint Your Wagon* (1951), *An American in Paris* (1951), *My Fair Lady* (1956), *Gigi* (1958) and *Camelot* (1962), Lerner at this time was under contract to Paramount to produce a total of five musical extravaganzas. . . . Extremely enthused, Lerner wrote a screenplay in the midst of production chores on *Paint Your Wagon* and *On a Clear Day You Can See Forever.*

Recalling that Frederick Loewe, Lerner's former collaborator and now a Palm Springs retiree, had independently expressed an interest in the work, Tandet sent him the scenario. Loewe was hooked immediately and began composing a score with Lerner (their first collaboration since the film version of *My Fair Lady* in 1964).

Robert Evans, Paramount's production vice-president, gave Saint Exupery's book to director Stanley Donen, one of the top builders of the Hollywood musical. . . . Donen . . . was quite touched by the Exupery work and equally eager to make another musical (his last had been *Damn Yankees* in 1958). Moreover, he had already collaborated with Alan Lerner — and quite successfully — when he replaced Charles Walters in the shooting of *Royal Wedding* in 1951.

Despite the fact that Donen's forte was the musical, in light of the resulting work, Jean-Pierre Coursodon's comment that "anyone who has read Saint-Exupery's [book] could have told [the director] that it would be almost impossible not to overproduce it, and that its fragile, whimsical charm was sure to be damaged, if not destroyed, by the literalness of film" is particularly applicable. The problem no doubt stemmed from the fact that *The Little Prince* marked Donen's first tackling of a literary adaptation;

all of his former superb musical films (among them *On the Town*, 1949, *Singin' in the Rain*, 1952, *Seven Brides for Seven Brothers*, 1954, *Funny Face*, 1957, and *The Pajama Game*, 1957) and non-musical efforts (such as *Charade*, 1964, *Arabesque*, 1966, and *Two for the Road*, 1967) had been original screenplays which were ideally suited to his stylistic temperament (albeit one which has been difficult to discern fully from that of his co-directors and choreographers like Gene Kelly, Bob Fosse and Michael Kidd).

In addition to being Lerner and Loewe's first musical in 13 years, it was also Donen's first since *The Pajama Game*. But unlike *Pajama Game*, *Prince* was a piece of material which already existed on its own as a straight dramatic work, one to which a musical treatment did not readily lend itself. So already Donen was limited in terms of artistic freedom by his desire to preserve the essential spirit of Saint-Exupery while imposing a familiar format upon it. Unfortunately, he was not aided by the score of Lerner and Loewe (their last), which, as Casper points out, was "derivative of their former successes, in particular *My Fair Lady*, *Gigi* and *Camelot*, [a factor that made it seem] anachronistic in the seventies . . . [and] also [which] failed to capture the poetic charm and rhythm of Saint Exupery's prose. Additionally, it failed to lend itself to dancing . . . this last shortcoming particularly affected Donen, whose forte was the dance musical.

Actually, much of the film resembles a children's fantasy-*opera*. The majority of the numbers feature the Pilot (Richard Kiley) expounding to himself on his dilemma in coming to terms with the Prince (Steven Warner) and his world. And indeed the visuals (mainly montages of the Pilot flying or racing across desert sands) seem to reinforce this impression, as they do not display a seamless integration of time and space but rather play against (by attempting to approximate in a too-painstaking way) the players' movements. This is related to the literalism of which Coursodon speaks. The constant emphasis on montage in detailing nearly all of the Prince's encounters with characters such as the Monarch (Joss Ackland), Businessman (Clive Revill), Scholar (Victor Spinnetti) and Rose (Donna McKechnie) soon becomes boring, in spite of the often striking location (Tozeur in

Gene Wilder as the Fox.

southern Tunisia on the edge of the Sahara Desert was chosen)
photography by Christopher Challis (whose work on the opening
village scenes recalls Billy Wilder's British-made *The Private Life
of Sherlock Holmes*, 1970, which Challis also photographed) and
art direction by Norman Reynolds and John Barry, utilizing
modern abstract sets which often verge on the surreal.

Oddly enough, the two numbers which stand out seem to
have been choreographed for another film entirely, despite the
emphasis on quick-cutting apparent in them. Indeed, Bob
Fosse's "Snake in the Grass" was worked out by him alone

Bob Fosse as the Snake.

(though Donen edited the sequence), and is the film's singular exhilarating scene. As the sinister snake, Fosse, bedecked with a python-trimmed black outfit and yellow-tinted specs, succeeds in creating an ingeniously flashy routine which reminds one of the modern style he brought to his film versions of the Broadway hits *Sweet Charity* (1969) and *Cabaret* (1972) as well as the original scenario *All That Jazz* (1979). The film's other highlight is Gene Wilder's "Closer and Closer and Closer," in which he, as the Fox, chases the Prince about in much the same manner as the Snake—and the *mise en scène* here is consistent too with that throughout the piece—only with friendly overtones this time.

Crucial to one's response to the film are Donen's choices for the leads, Richard Kiley as the Pilot and Steven Warner as the Prince. Kiley, an expert baritone, comes off better, mainly because of his many years of experience as both actor and singer— but although he manages to convey the Pilot's self-discovery with a good deal of charisma, one cannot help but wonder how much better the other, greater, actors such as Richard Burton and Richard Harris would have been in the role—in particular Frank Sinatra, who initially expressed interest but whom Donen decided against because the director felt Sinatra could not be counted on to commit to the project before the deadline. Steven Warner is largely unsatisfactory—mainly due to an irritating lisp which causes him to garble many of his lines—but he does possess an innate sense of timing which serves him particularly well in reacting to Kiley's befuddlement (the fact that the six-year-old was British no doubt was the cause of the latter trait). Still, one cannot help but feel that the choice was at least in part a lazy one on the part of Donen, and indeed, he confessed to Casper that the reason he chose Warner was he simply couldn't bear to audition any more children.

The Little Prince was a miserable flop upon its release in 1974, perhaps due to Paramount's emphasis on marketing Coppola's epic *Godfather II*, the studio's sure-fire Oscar contender which was released at the same time (the studio gave the same lackluster treatment to Peter Bogdanovich's *Daisy Miller*, also released in 1974, another literary adaptation which, coincidentally, also suffered from the same problem of literalism as *Prince*). Although it is revived on television, it has not achieved any kind of belated classic status as a film of a Saint Exupery work, nor is it regarded as one of Stanley Donen's best pictures. It remains a failed, though not entirely negligible, entertainment which is of more interest to adults who can appreciate the sporadic artistry of its collaborators and the nobility of their efforts than to children who need to be excited constantly and couldn't give a damn for so-called "sophisticated" fare.

The Slipper and the Rose: The Story of Cinderella

A Paradine Co-Production, *released by* Universal, 1976. *Producer* Stuart Lyons. *Executive Producer* David Frost. *Director* Bryan Forbes. *Screenplay by* Bryan Forbes and Robert B. and Richard M. Sherman. *Director of Photography* Tony Imi, B.S.C. *Production Designer* Ray Simm. *Editor* Timothy Gee. *Costume Designer* Julie Harris. *Choreographer* Marc Breaux. *Music Arranged and Conducted by* Angela Morley. *Production Coordinators* Naim Attallah, Jim Asperg. *Assistant to the Producer* John L. Hargreaves. *Production Supervisor* Peter Manley. *Camera Operator* Tony White. *Sound Recording* Bill Daniels. *Assistant Directors* Jack Causey, Richard Jenkins, John Downes, Leonhard Gmur. *Continuity* Penny Daniels. *Sound Editor* Janet Davidson. *Music Editor* Bob Hathaway. *Sound Mixer* Gordon McCallum. *Music Mixer* Eric Tomlinson. *Art Director* Bert Davey. *Titles* Robert Ellis. *Special Effects* Roy Capel. *Boom Operator* Gus Lloyd. *Focus Puller* George Watts. *Camera Grip* Colin Manning. *Chief Hairdresser* Barbara Ritchie. *Chief Makeup* Basil Newall. *Wardrobe Supervisor* Brenda Dabbs. *Wardrobe Master* John Hilling. *Wardrobe Mistress* Eileen Sullivan. *Makeup* Paul Rabiger. *Set Dresser* Jack Stephens. *Props* Paddy Bennett. *Construction Manager* Bill Waldron. *Assistant Choreographer* Suzanne France. *Electrical Supervisor* Bert Bosher. *Clapper/Loader* Beaumont Alexander. *Sound Camera Operator* Peter Desbois. *Sound Maintenance* Bob Taylor. *Location Managers* Ian Goddard, Dietmar Siegert. *Stills* George Courtney Ward. *Hairdressers* Lithne Fennell, Joan White. *Wardrobe Assistants* Jo Osmond, Ken Lawson. *Assistant Editor* Graham Farrow. *Assistant Music Editor* Ken Ross. *Vocal Coach* Jim Walker. *Production Buyer* Harry Parr. *Casting Director* Michael Barnes. *Publicity* Geoff Freeman, Fred Hift & Associates. *Production Accountant* John Collingwood. *Production Secretaries* Ann Thrift, Jean Walter. *Costumes* Bermans & Nathans, Jean Bennett, Shirley Reid, Arthur Davey. *Wigs* Simon Wigs Ltd. Panavision. Technicolor. Running Time: 128 minutes.

Cast Richard Chamberlain (Prince), Gemma Craven (Cinderella), Kenneth More (Chamberlain), Michael Hordern (King), Edith Evans (Dowager Queen), Annette Crosbie (Fairy Godmother), Margaret Lockwood (Stepmother), Christopher Gable (John), Julian Orchard (Montague), Lally Bowers (Queen), John Turner (Major Demo), Sherrie Hewson (Palatine), Rosalind Ayres (Isobella), Keith Skinner (Willoughby), Polly Williams (Lady Caroline), Norman Bird (Dress Shop Proprietor), Roy Barraclough (Tailor), Elizabeth Mansfield (Lady in Waiting to Queen), Peter Graves (General), Gerald Sim (1st Lord of Navy), Geoffrey Balydon (Archbishop), Valentine Dyell (2nd Major Demo), Tim Barrett (Minister), Vivienne McKee (Bride), Andre Movel (Bride's Father), Myrtle Reed (Bride's Mother), Ludmilla Nova (2nd Lady in Waiting to Queen), Peter Leeming (Singing Guard), Marianne Broom, Tessa Dahl, Lea Dregorn, Eva Reuber-Staler, Ann Rutherford, Suzette St. Claire (Princesses), Jenny Lee Wright (Milk Maid), Patrick Jordan, Rocky Taylor (Prince's Guards), Paul Schmitzburger (Cow Herd).

Music and Lyrics by Richard M. and Robert B. Sherman: "Why Can't I Be Two People," "Once I Was Loved," "What a Comforting Thing to Know," "Protocoli-Gorically Correct," "He Danced with Me, She Danced with Me," "Bride Finding Ball," "Suddenly it Happens," "Slipper and the Rose Waltz," "Secret Kingdom," "Position and Positioning," "Tell Him Anything."

The Slipper and the Rose, like *Alice's Adventures in Wonderland,* an almost exclusively British production, was eagerly anticipated upon its release in 1976 as the film which would bring about a renaissance of the children's musical. As I have noted, most of the other entries of recent years (such as *Alice* and *Wonka*) had vanished from sight after a short theatrical run, and other, bigger-budget films like *Bedknobs* and *Chitty,* while highly publicized, had performed less than spectacularly at the box office than had been expected—as well as being, for the most part, critical failures as well.

Unfortunately, *The Slipper and the Rose* was not to alter that trend. While opulent in terms of production design and photography, and although it boasts, like *Alice,* a roster of some of the finest acting talents in Britain (including Sir Michael Hordern, Kenneth More, Christopher Gable and 87-year-old Edith Evans, making her last screen appearance), it remains stubbornly—even determinedly—uninventive and unexciting in terms of treatment.

This result certainly contradicted the original intentions of Bryan Forbes, who directed and co-wrote the film:

> I felt that the Cinderella legend was a perennial favourite for children of all ages but that it had often been reduced to its bare bones and tackled without any humour. Therefore, I attempted to inject some new blood into old veins and wherever possible tried to give the characters substance rather than shadow, tried to make them human and believable and at the same time invented a fictitious country that would serve as a credible background to the basic legend.

Unfortunately, much of the reason Forbes was hampered in his approach had to do with the screenplay by the Sherman Brothers submitted to him (it was their second—the first had been for their forgettable musicalization of *Tom Sawyer* in 1973) which, he says, he revised in ten days' time. Judging from the result, he was not able to improve it much. It seems that Forbes' ideas about breathing new life into a time-worn story had been lost on the Shermans when they set out to fashion a live-action musical from the *Cinderella* tales. That they would have done so in the first place is particularly surprising considering that they were Disney veterans, and no doubt realized that most people's memories of the tale were associated solely with Disney's 1949 animated feature, which, while not his best work, remains very charming and magical and miles ahead of all other competition before or since.

Apparently their aim was to focus exclusively on the human characters (largely neglected in the cartoon in favor of the mice and other creatures—by far the highlights of the piece), since this was to be a live-action film (though at one point a group of actors dressed in mice suits are seen, for no very good reason, and are dispensed with quickly—a reminder of the embarrassing costumes in *Alice*). So as a result we are immediately introduced to the Prince (Richard Chamberlain) and his dilemma over finding a suitable wife. The episodes with him are alternated with those involving Cinderella (Gemma Craven) for the duration of this seemingly endless enterprise. The Disney version had wisely

Cinderella (Gemma Craven) and her Fairy Godmother.

jettisoned plot (acknowledging that this was an exceedingly simple story) in favor of numerous episodes involving the mice and cat. Unable to focus on critters, the Shermans obviously intended to flesh out the people as much as possible, and therefore found it necessary to lengthen their scenario. But they forgot to add dimension to or flesh out any of the characters, so as a result all we're left with is a gallery of people about for whom one is never given any particularly good reason to care. There is very little real humor throughout, just a lot of incorrigible old stiffs blathering about how the Prince's indecisions are affecting their lives.

This would seem lackluster enough, but the Shermans decided to puff up the proceedings even more with a gallery of completely useless and just plain awful songs—the quality of which pales even more when compared to the inspired ditties (such as "Work Song," "A Dream Is a Wish Your Heart Makes" and "Bibbidy Bobbidy Boo") by Mack David, Jerry Livingston

The "Protocoli-Gorically Correct" number.

and Al Hoffman which were featured in the animated version. The film plods on for a whopping *two hours and eight minutes* (incredibly, the British version is 18 minutes *longer*—I shudder to think what's missing)—and even after the slipper situation is resolved, the story is extended further by the ridiculous introduction of a subplot in which the King insists that Cinderella, because a commoner, would be an unsuitable bride for his son in the eve of war; he attempts to arrange a marriage of alliance. But, of course, in the end good triumphs over evil and the Prince gets his way.

One should not blame the Shermans *entirely*, however, for Bryan Forbes, whose first musical this was, was not really the ideal choice for director either. Although his career had started with a film about childhood innocence, *Whistle Down the Wind* (1961), which, as he himself acknowledges, has become "something of a minor classic," the delicacy required for a children's musical piece was not suited to the writer-director of the hard-edged POW drama *King Rat* (1965), his best effort (this was to be proven definitively two years after *Slipper* with the release of Forbes' sequel to 1944's *National Velvet*, *International Velvet*, an incoherent and grossly sentimental effort). In the case of *Slipper*, Forbes' major shortcoming was his fatal inability to inject any semblance of *life* into the proceedings — certainly he had the cast and settings to enable him to at least make the Shermans' unsurprising material *look* exciting, or at least interesting. Richard Chamberlain gives it his all as the Prince, making him seem something more than the standard cardboard good-looking leading man, but he is not enough to save the production. Gemma Craven is a pretty and willing Cinderella, but not much else.

The other technical contributions are largely disappointing also, among them the special effects — one would have expected the team at the very least to have tried to duplicate the effects in the animated version (such as the pumpkin turning into a coach), but even those have been neglected. And if one has been interested in trying to discern the individual contributions of choreographers Breaux and Wood to the efforts discussed thus far, he need look no further than this film, which was helmed by Breaux exclusively — the results are a series of disheveled routines which never even approach the electricity which Wood apparently gave to the team's work in the earlier films (an ability no doubt gleaned from her pre–Breaux effort with Michael Kidd, *Lil' Abner*, 1959). As it stands, only Chamberlain and Ray Simm's sets may sustain one through the duration. Alas.

Pete's Dragon

A Walt Disney Productions presentation, *released by* Buena Vista Distribution Corporation, 1977. *Producers* Ron Miller and Jerome Courtland. *Director* Don Chaffey. *Screenplay* Malcolm Marmorstein, *based on a story by* Seton I. Miller and S.S. Field. *Director of Photography* Frank Phillips, A.S.C. *Choreography* Onna White. *Music Arranged, Supervised and Conducted by* Irwin Kostal. *Art Directors* John B. Mansbridge, Jack Martin Smith. *Editor* Gordon D. Brenner. *Costumes* Bill Thomas. *Associate Choreographer* Martin Allen. *Dance Arranger* David Baker. *Set Decorator* Lucien M. Hafley. *Matte Artwork* P.S. Ellenshaw. *Special Effects* Eustace Lycett, A. Cruickshank, A.S.C., Danny Lee. *Effects Animator* Morse A. Lanpher. *Associate Animation Supervisor* Chuck Williams. *Elliot created by* Ken Anderson. *Animation Director* Don Bluth. *Animation Art Director* Ken Anderson. *Layout* Joe Hale. *Character Animation* John Pomeroy, Gary Goldman, Chuck Harvey, Ron Clement, Bill Hajee, Randy Cartwright, Glen Keane, Cliff Nordberg. *Production Manager* John Bloss. *Unit Production Manager* Christopher Seiter. *Assistant Director* Ronald R. Grow. *2nd Assistant Director* John M. Poer. *Script Supervisor* Herb Taylor. *Sound Mixer* Frank C. Regula. *Stunt Coordinator* John Moio. *Costume Coordinators* Chuck Keehne, Emily Sundby. *Makeup* Robert J. Schuffer. *Hairstyles* LaRue Matheron. *Sound Editor* Raymond Craddock. *Animation Editor* James Melton. *Music Editor* Evelyn Kennedy. Technicolor. Running Time: 128 minutes.

Cast Helen Reddy (Nora), Jim Dale (Dr. Terminus), Mickey Rooney (Lampie), Red Buttons (Hoagy), Shelley Winters (Lena Gogan), Sean Marshall (Pete), Jane Kean (Miss Taylor), Jim Backus (Mayor), Charles Tyner (Merle), Jeff Conaway (Willie), Gary Morgan (Grover), Cal Bartlett (Paul), Charlie Callas (Voice of Elliott), Walter Barnes (Captain), Al Checco (Fisherman 1), Henry Slate (Fisherman 2), Jack Collins (Fisherman 3), Robert Eaton (Stone Proprietor), Roger Price (Man With Visor), Robert Foulk (Old Sea Captain), Ben Wrigley (Egg Man), Joe Ross (Cementman).

Sean Marshall, Mickey Rooney, Helen Reddy and Cal Bartlett bid farewell to the dragon.

Music and Lyrics by Al Kasha and Joel Hirschorn: "I Saw a Dragon," "It's Not Easy," "Candle on the Water," "Every Little Piece," "The Happiest Home in These Hills," "Brazzle Dazzle Day," "Boo Bop Bopbop Bop (I Love You, Too)," "There's Room for Everyone," "Passamashloddy," "Bill of Sale."

It is sad to have to end this volume with what is undoubtedly the most incompetent entry yet in the genre of chidren's live-action musicals. Not surprisingly, the feature, *Pete's Dragon*, was yet another product of the Disney people following the death of Walt. It is perhaps the ultimate expression of the something-for-everyone, nothing-for-anyone-with-taste motto. Scripts for the previous Disney live-action films were almost always very poor, but this time there is no attention at all given to plot or character development. The scenario, a kind of juvenile rewrite of *Harvey*, is an extraordinarily disheveled and pointless series of arbitrary

Jim Dale (left) and Red Buttons entice Sean Marshall.

episodes surrounding the arrival of a small boy named Pete (Sean Marshall), whose only companion is a pet dragon which only he can see, in a small town in Maine in 1900 following his escape from grasping foster parents.

For some two hours after this, not much else happens except that several characters, such as a local maiden (Helen Reddy) who pines for her husband who has apparently been lost at sea, her father (Mickey Rooney) and his drinking buddy (Red Buttons), and a few others are introduced, then sort of shuffled about for an eternity—interspersed with the obligatory awful physical antics resulting from the townspeople's not being able to see the dragon—until a sudden climax wherein the dragon somehow causes a storm to bring the maiden's husband back, and in which the dragon leaves to help others, the boy apparently having found a home in the village and outwitted his greedy foster parents.

The script is full of ridiculous incongruities and situations and stock characters. Particularly lamentable is the Helen Reddy character, who prances about singing all kinds of bouncy tunes about a hopeful tomorrow and acting as though she really believes Pete's dragon exists, only to have us discover in the final minutes that she is genuinely surprised when the creature finally reveals itself to her. And there is a gross inconsistency in the fact that Reddy's father and his friends are able to see the dragon; it would have made much more sense to have it only visible to Pete, so that his psychological motivations for needing it could have been explored—the *Mary Poppins*ish ending tacked on by the scenarists in which Pete decides he no longer needs the dragon seems thoroughly unmotivated, since we were never shown the boy (as we were in *Poppins* with the two children) before the dragon came into his life, and also know nothing about his past.

Still more lamentable is that a cast of excellent actors (including Mickey Rooney, Shelley Winters and Red Buttons) has been wasted on laughable material which calls for them to mug-mug and dress up in costumes which their high school drama teachers would have found embarrassing. The fact that Sean Marshall plays it straight and makes us believe that there is a dragon there is wasted by the fact that, unlike in *Harvey*, the creature is *not* a figment of his imagination.

This leads to the most disastrous aspect of the production—and the one on which most of the money was apparently spent—namely the interaction of the animated dragon with the live-action and the drawing of the dragon itself. Except for a few moments, the thing looks pasted on, and is pretty limited in terms of movement, reminding one of critic Barry Took's comment that the result looks "like the work of the Burbank Amateur Camera Club." Incidentally, the format of combining live-action and animation displayed herein and in the past Disney features (in which a stationary camera was employed and the animation merely accommodated) has been rendered obsolete forever by the 1988 release of *Who Framed Roger Rabbit*, a revolutionary work masterminded by director Robert Zemeckis and animator Richard Williams (and, interestingly, backed by Disney's subsidiary, Touchstone) in which a new process known as multi-generational character interaction was pioneered. For the first time in history, animated characters and live actors shared the same space as Zemeckis and company devised a method for keeping the camera moving constantly, subordinating itself, as it were, to the whims of the animated figures, who stepped in and out of frame, leapt about, and performed all kinds of amazing physical stunts while being rendered three-dimensional by the innovative use of light and shadow. As a matter of fact, one of the creative personnel involved with *Roger Rabbit* commented that *Pete's Dragon*, in terms of animation, has always been used as the example of what *not* to do.

In conclusion, the genre discussed herein has really come to a close. Studios are much more inclined to spend big bucks (which this type of film requires) on vulgar comedies with top-name stars than on innocent fare whose appeal is limited mainly to Saturday matinees. Children's fare nowadays is mainly confined to the abysmal Saturday-morning and weekday cartoons to be found on local TV stations across the country. Occasionally, there are stabs at live-action, but these are usually done as TV miniseries, not feature films. The two most prominent ones in recent years have been 1986's *Babes in Toyland* (with a score by Leslie Bricusse) and 1985's *Alice in Wonderland*. I have noted the disastrous quality of the former effort earlier, and as for the latter, despite an all-star cast it turned out to be even more interminable and unmagical than *Alice's Adventures in Wonderland*. But there is one consolation for all: the immortal *Wizard of Oz* continues to be shown annually on commercial television, and is available for purchase on videocassette as well (and has been a bestseller, needless to say).

Bibliography

"Alice's Adventures in Wonderland," in *London Times*, July 30, 1972, p. 34.

Atkins, Irene Kahn. "The Wizard of Oz," in *Magill's Survey of Cinema*, Vol. 1. Englewood Cliffs, N.J.: Salem Press, 1980.

Burke, John. *Chitty Chitty Bang Bang, The Story of the Film*, based on the screenplay by Roald Dahl and Ken Hughes from Ian Fleming's original stories. London: Pan Books, 1968.

Coursodon, Jeanne-Pierre. "Richard Fleischer" and "Stanley Donen" in *American Directors*, Vol. 2. New York: McGraw-Hill, 1983. pp. 132–138, 99–109.

Crowther, Bosley. "Hans Christian Andersen" in *New York Times*, November 26, 1952, p. 20.

Dahl, Roald. *Charlie and the Chocolate Factory*. New York: Alfred A. Knopf, 1964.

Dunne, John Gregory. *The Studio*. New York: Farrar, Straus & Giroux, 1969.

Einstein, Donald. "The 5000 Fingers of Dr. T," in *Magill's Survey of Cinema*, Vol. 2. Englewood Cliffs, N.J.: Salem Press, 1981.

Freedland, Michael. *The Secret Life of Danny Kaye*. New York: St. Martin's Press, 1985.

Goldwyn, Samuel. "Goldwyn's Fairy Tale Dream Comes True," in *New York Times*, October 23, 1952, sec. 4, p. 3.

Halliwell, Leslie. *Halliwell's Film and Video Guide*, 6th Edition. New York: Charles Scribners Sons, 1987.

Harmetz, Aljean. *The Making of the Wizard of Oz*. New York: Limelight Editions, 1984.

Hickman, G.M. *The Films of George Pal*. South Brunswick, N.J.: A.S. Barnes, 1977.

Kael, Pauline. *5001 Nights at the Movies*. New York: Holt, Rinehart and Winston, 1982.

_____. *Kiss Kiss Bang Bang*. New York: Holt, Rinehart and Winston, 1971.

Lyon, Christopher, editor. *The International Directory of Films and Filmmakers*, Vol. 2. New York: Putnam, 1984.

Maltin, Leonard. *The Disney Films*. New York: Bonanza Books, 1973.

Marill, Alvin H. *Samuel Goldwyn Presents*. Cranbury, N.J.: A.S. Barnes, 1975.

Marx, Arthur. *Goldwyn: A Biography of the Man Behind the Myth*. New York: W.W. Norton, 1976.

McClelland, Doug. *Down the Yellow Brick Road: The Making of the Wizard of Oz*. New York: Pyramid Books, 1976.

Peary, Danny, editor and author. *Cult Movies*, Vols. 1 & 2. New York: Dell, 1981, 1983.

Pratley, Gerald. *The Cinema of Otto Preminger*. New York: A.S. Barnes, 1971.

"Pufnstuf" review in *Variety*, June 3, 1970, Vol. 259, No. 3, p. 17.

Spoto, Donald. *Stanley Kramer: Film Maker*. New York: G.P. Putnam's Sons, 1978.

Street, Douglas, editor. *Children's Novels and the Movies*. New York: Frederick Ungar, 1983.

Videography

(Abbreviation codes follow the Videography.)

Title	35mm	16mm	Video
The Wizard of Oz	MGM/UA	FI	MGM/UA V
Hans Christian Andersen	G		EHV
The 5000 Fingers of Dr. T	C	FI	n.a.
tom thumb	MGM/UA	FI	MGM/UA
Babes in Toyland	WD	n.a.	WDHV
Mary Poppins	WD	n.a.	WDHV
Doctor Dolittle	20th		CBS/FOX
Chitty Chitty Bang Bang	MGM/UA	FI	CBS/FOX
Pufnstuf	U	n.a.	n.a.
Bedknobs and Broom-sticks	WD	n.a.	WDHV
Willy Wonka	WB	FI	WHV
Alice's Adventures in Wonderland	20th	FI	Playhouse
The Little Prince	P		PHV
The Slipper and the Rose	U	n.a.	n.a.
Pete's Dragon	WD	n.a.	WDHV

Abbreviation Codes*

C	Columbia Pictures, Columbia Plaza West, Burbank, Ca. 91505 (818) 954-6000
CBS/FOX	CBS/FOX Video
EHV	Embassy Home Video
FI	Films Incorporated, toll-free number: (800) 223-6246

G	Samuel Goldwyn Company, 10203 Santa Monica Blvd., Los Angeles, Ca. 90046 (213) 552-2255
MGM/UA	MGM/United Artists, 10202 W. Washington Blvd., Culver City, Ca. (213) 280-6000
MGM/UA V	MGM/UA Home Video
P	Paramount Pictures, 5555 Melrose Ave., Los Angeles, Ca. 90038 (213) 468-5000
PHV	Paramount Home Video
Playhouse	Playhouse Video
20th	20th Century-Fox, 10201 W. Pico Blvd., Los Angeles, Ca. 90035 (213) 277-2211
U	Universal Pictures, 100 Universal City Plaza, Universal City, Ca. 91608 (818) 777-1000
WB	Warner Brothers, 4000 Warner Blvd., Burbank, Ca. 91522 (818) 954-6000
WD	The Walt Disney Company, 500 S. Buena Vista, Burbank, Ca. 91522 (818) 840-1000
WDHV	Walt Disney Home Video
WHV	Warner Home Video

"n.a." means not available.

Index